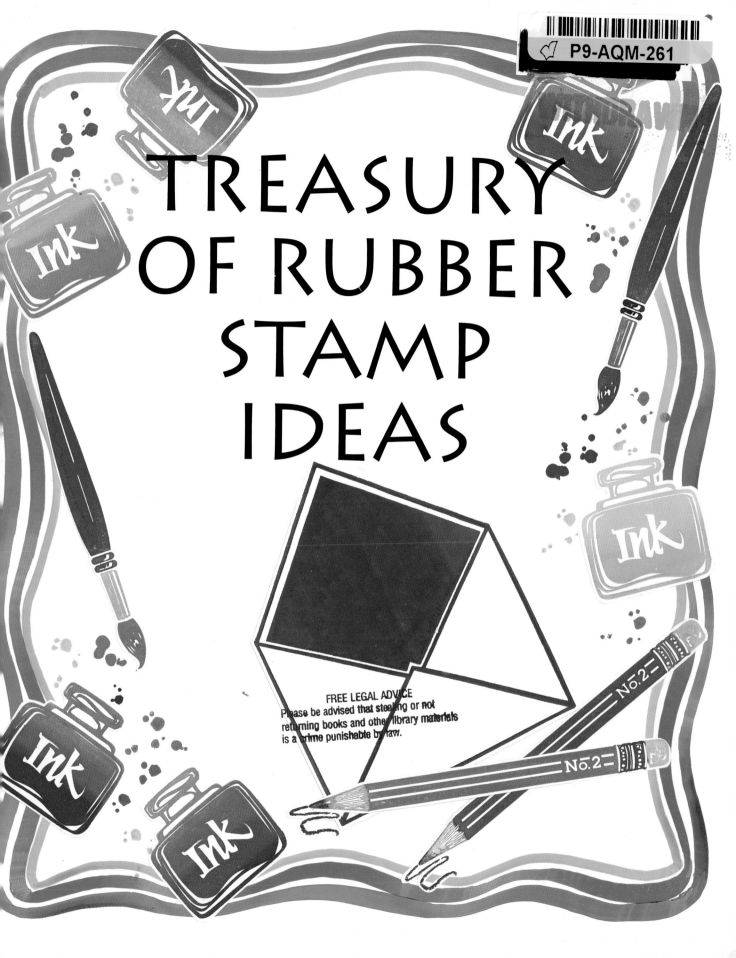

TREASURY OF RUBBER STAMP IDEAS

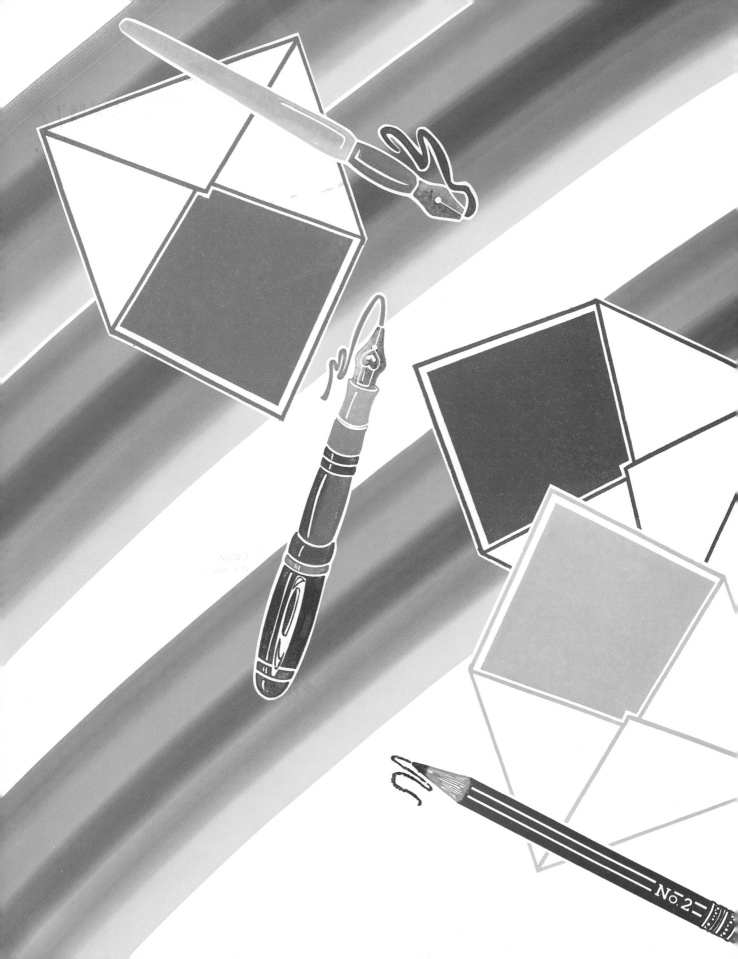

TREASURY
OF RUBBER
STAMP
IDEAS

Dee Gruenig

Sterling Publishing Co., Inc. New York
A Sterling / Chapelle Book

Chapelle:
- Jo Packham, Owner
- Cathy Sexton, Editor
- Staff: Marie Barber, Ann Bear, Areta Bingham, Kass Burchett, Rebecca Christensen, Holly Fuller, Marilyn Goff, Shirley Heslop, Holly Hollingsworth, Shawn Hsu, Susan Jorgensen, Pauline Locke, Barbara Milburn, Linda Orton, Karmen Quinney, Leslie Ridenour, and Cindy Stoeckl

Photography:
- Kevin Dilley, Photographer for Hazen Photography
- Kass Burchett, Photo Stylist for Chapelle

The author would like to thank the following companies and manufacturers for providing materials that were used in this publication: Burns & Allen, C-Thru Ruler, Clearsnap, Enchanted Creations, Family Treasures, Fiskar, Ivory Coast, Loew Cornell, Mark Enterprises, Marvy Uchida, Mrs. Grossman's Paper Co., Neil Enterprises, Posh Impressions, Ranger Industries, Rubber Stampede, Sakura Color Products, Savoir Faire, Speedball Mfg., Tsukineko, Union Rubber, and Xyron.

If you have any questions or comments, please contact Chapelle, Ltd., Inc., P.O. Box 9252, Ogden, UT 84409 •
(801) 621-2777 • (801) 621-2788 Fax • e-mail: Chapelle1@aol.com

To Mom, with much love, for encouraging me to pursue my passion in fine arts and for teaching me to appreciate things that have true value and deeper meaning.

My heartfelt thanks to my creative support staff, without which this book would not have been possible — Lynne Taylor, Vicki Sullivan, Jill Ham, Carey Cannon, Betty Waldeck, and Shari Kowalke.

About the Author

Dee Gruenig is widely known as the head cheerleader of rubber stamping and has been called the "Renoir of Rubber." She has solid qualifications to write about the subject, with extensive experience as innovator, teacher, retailer, motivator, and leader in both the craft and gift industries.

As innovator, she has adapted numerous accessories to make original stamping effects possible. She also popularized the novel idea of applying a colored marker directly to a stamp's rubber surface, thereby making easy the exact placement of color for precise detail and control—something not possible with a stamp pad.

As teacher, she was first to popularize stamping to large audiences. She has taught approximately 30,000 students personally and many more through four popular videos and four successful books. Additionally, she teaches rubber stamping to art and craft instructors of the United States Army in the U.S. and abroad.

As retailer, she established long-running sales records for major fund raisers that led to the establishment of two stores plus holiday stores in major shopping malls.

As motivator, she was first to introduce rubber stamps to millions on television in 1989. She has since appeared numerous times on popular craft television shows. On television, she has represented products other than her own and other retailers employ her regularly to get their own customers enthusiastic about this enjoyable and useful activity.

As an industry leader, she has served on two major advisory boards and is currently serving on the Hobby Industry Association's (HIA) Board of Directors.

Nearly twenty years of varied experience, sustained dedication, and the love of rubber stamping are evident within the covers of this book!

Contents

GENERAL INSTRUCTIONS

Basic Stamping

Always start with a clean, dry rubber stamp. When using rubber stamps for the first time, it is often necessary to rough up the rubber design area of the stamp with a pumice sponge to remove any leftover silicone from the manufacturing process. This will assure a smooth, clear colored impression rather than a splotchy or speckled one.

Always stamp on a flat, padded surface, such as a magazine or stack of paper, that is larger than the project being stamped. This will assure an even impression of the entire image.

To ink the rubber stamp, press it onto a stamp pad with ink for one-color stamping or color it with markers for multicolor stamping. If desired, blend the colors, from light to dark. Then go over the line where the colors meet with the lighter color to blend smoothly.

For bright images, press the rubber stamp carefully, but firmly onto coated (glossy) paper or cardstock. Make certain to apply even pressure to the stamp — the larger the stamp, the more pressure required for a good impression. To prevent smearing, lift the rubber stamp straight up.

When stamping images onto sticker paper to make stickers, cut out leaving a $1/16"$ border.

Embossing

Embossing powders are available in many opaque colors, as well as metallic, irridescent, and sparklers, which contain glitter.

Heat tools are made for embossing. They get very hot, but they do not blow much air. The air blown from a hair dryer is too forceful, therefore it will not work as an embossing heat tool.

To begin, gather the following supplies:
- Porous, non-coated paper or cardstock
- Pigment ink pad(s)
- Rubber stamp(s)
- Embossing powder(s)
- Heat tool

Cover your working space with paper to protect it from the excess ink and embossing powder that is applied to the paper or cardstock.

Apply pigment ink to the design area of a rubber stamp by dabbing a pigment ink pad onto it. Apply it evenly in two directions to avoid missing any areas of the design. Once the pigment ink covers the entire rubber design, stamp directly onto the paper or cardstock with firm, even pressure. Make certain to avoid too much pressure as this will cause the ink to smear or blur.

Lift the stamp straight up and immediately apply embossing powder to the stamped image. Use the embossing powder liberally and shake off the excess back into the jar.

Next, heat the powdered image with a heat tool until all areas are "melted."

Finally, clean the rubber stamp thoroughly with stamp cleaner or water mixed with a little window cleaner.

Brayering with a Soft Rubber Brayer

The soft rubber brayer is the most commonly used brayer and is available in 2", 4", and 6" widths.

To begin, gather the following supplies:
- Coated paper or cardstock
- Stamp pad(s) or colored markers
- Rubber stamp(s)
- Soft rubber brayer

This technique is used for creating backgrounds and reverse rubber stamp images.

Cover your working space with paper to protect it from the excess ink that is applied to the paper or cardstock.

For reverse rubber stamp images, apply ink to a rubber stamp, using colored markers, and lay it down on a flat, padded surface with the inked side up. Roll a soft rubber brayer over the rubber stamp, one or two times, making certain to start and end off either side of the image so the entire image ends up on the brayer. It may be necessary to "exhale" on the rubber stamp to remoisten the residue ink before you roll across the rubber stamp the second time.

Depending on the image, you may also choose to change the angle or position the second time.

Repeat and re-ink as necessary for the desired effect.

For deeper color, stamp freshly colored images. The brayered images will be lighter in intensity and reversed from the stamped images. For an all-over pattern, various angles and positions are recommended. For landscapes, you would want the trees and leaves to vary only slightly.

Stripes or patterns can also be drawn directly on the rubber with markers.

Finally, clean the brayer with stamp cleaner or water mixed with a little window cleaner.

Brayering with a Sponge Brayer

The sponge brayer is made from a soft sponge material and has a plastic handle, therefore, these brayers are very inexpensive.

To begin, gather the following supplies:
- Coated paper or cardstock
- Colored markers
- Sponge brayer
- Spray bottle of water

This technique is used for creating backgrounds with a watercolor effect.

Cover your working space with paper to protect it from the excess ink that is applied to the paper or cardstock.

Color the surface of the sponge brayer in random patterns with several colors of markers for the desired effect.

Lightly spray the surface of the sponge brayer with two or three sprays from a spray bottle of water. Roll the sponge brayer directly over the paper or cardstock.

Repeat and re-ink as necessary for the desired effect.

Do not be alarmed if the paper should curl from the water, it will dry virtually flat.

Finally, clean the brayer with water and squeeze out excess before changing colors.

Brayering with a Black Foam Brayer

The black foam brayer is made from a hard-textured sponge-type material, and because of its texture, a softer look is rendered.

To begin, gather the following supplies:

- Coated paper or cardstock
- Rainbow pad(s) or colored markers
- Black foam brayer

This technique is used for creating backgrounds with a rainbow effect.

Cover your working space with paper to protect it from the excess ink that is applied to the paper or cardstock.

Ink the entire surface of the black foam brayer by rolling it from front to back over a rainbow pad. Roll the brayer six to eight times to thoroughly saturate the brayer with color.

If desired, markers can also be used to color the black foam brayer.

Roll the inked brayer back and forth in the same area of the paper or cardstock several times beginning and ending off the page.

Repeat and re-ink as necessary for the desired effect.

Turn the paper or cardstock around and repeat the process matching the end colors.

Spray the brayer with water to create the watercolor effect.

Finally, clean the brayer with water.

Sponging with a Compressed Sponge

The compressed sponge starts out as a large sponge, but is compressed down to about 2" x 2" x 1". Because of its density, it holds a lot of ink.

To begin, gather the following supplies:
- Coated paper or cardstock
- Re-inker(s) or colored markers
- Compressed sponge

This technique is used for creating backgrounds and patterns with a streaked effect.

Cover your working space with paper to protect it from the excess ink that is applied to the paper or cardstock.

Apply ink to both sides of one corner edge of a compressed sponge with re-inkers or colored markers. It is best to use colors that will blend nicely like pink to purple to blue, or yellow to orange to brown.

The compressed sponge will absorb quite a lot of ink. Pull the inked edge of the sponge across the paper or cardstock starting and stopping off the edges for a continuous flow of color. Try straight, curved, or wavy lines, or perpendicular lines to create plaids.

Repeat and re-ink as necessary for the desired effect.

Finally, clean the sponge with water, but the colors will permanently stain it. If desired, the sponge does not need to be cleaned. Once the ink is dry the sponge can be designated for that color and each edge can be used for different colors.

Sponging with a Wedge Sponge

The wedge sponge, commonly known as a cosmetic or makeup sponge, can be used with colored markers to create several effects. A good quality sponge is important.

To begin, gather the following supplies:
- Coated paper or cardstock
- Colored markers
- Wedge sponge

This technique is used for creating backgrounds with varied effects.

Cover your working space with paper to protect it from the excess ink that is applied to the paper or cardstock.

Color one edge of the wedge sponge and lightly blot to test the intensity of the color.

To create an airbrushed effect, dab the sponge around the edge of the paper or cardstock. To render a darker color, dab over and over without blotting.

To create a streaked effect, place the sponge down on the paper or cardstock and pull it across the page.

Repeat and re-ink as necessary for the desired effect.

Finally, clean the sponge with water, but the colors will permanently stain it. If desired, the sponge does not need to be cleaned. Once the ink is dry the sponge can be designated for that color.

Spattering with a Twisting Spatter Brush

The twisting spatter brush is a circular brush with a wire handle, resembling a bottle brush. Attached to the handle is a wooden shuttle, with a wire rod extending into the bristles, through which the handle is turned.

To begin, gather the following supplies:
- Paper or cardstock
- Bottled ink
- Twisting spatter brush

This technique is used for creating backgrounds with bold streaked lines and for enhancing artwork with a "spattered" ink effect.

Cover your working space with paper to protect it from the excess ink that is applied to the paper or cardstock.

Dip the twisting spatter brush into bottled ink and tap off the excess ink.

To create bold streaked lines, hold back the wooden shuttle on the handle with the rod out of the bristles and drag the bristles over the paper, starting and ending off the edge. To spatter ink over artwork, hold the wooden shuttle and turn the wire handle.

Repeat and re-ink as necessary for the desired effect.

Finally, clean the brush with water.

Choosing an Appropriate Adhesive

There are several adhesives available that serve the same basic purpose. The type of adhesive that you choose should be based on personal preference, availability, and the project being created.

• Spray Adhesive:
Spray adhesive comes in a can and is considered permanent. Once the artwork or photo is mounted on the background it cannot be removed.

• Glue Pen:
Glue pens have various styles of tip applicators, which make them ideal when working with specific sized artwork or photos. Glue pens dispense a tacky glue that is easy to reposition when necessary.

• Tape and
Double-Sided Tabs:
Tape and double-sided tabs are best used with heavier papers because lightweight papers taped together might have a ridge from the tape.

• Rubber Cement:
Rubber cement is a popular adhesive because the excess can be "rolled" into a ball and comes off the page easily.

• Xyron™ Machine:
This machine allows an adhesive backing to be put onto any piece of paper or cardstock.

GALLERY OF STAMPED PROJECTS

Single-Window Photo Frame Cards

SINGLE-WINDOW PHOTO FRAME CARDS

Shown on pages 19-24.

These photo frame cards can be made in any size, but all those shown measure 6" x 9" for a folded card size of 6" x 4½" and are used both vertically and horizontally. They have been made from cardstock because it folds well and can withstand the weight of the stamped embellishments.

To begin, the size of the card must be determined. Once the cardstock has been cut and folded, any background can be applied over the cardstock on one or both sides as desired.

Because these are photo frame cards, a frame is then stamped or embossed directly onto the cardstock or stamped or embossed onto sticker paper, cut out, and adhered to the cardstock. Once the inside of the frame has been cut out and removed, the frame (window) will accentuate the

Sunflower Boy Card

Shown at right and on pages 19 & 21.

- Shown smaller than actual size.
- Cut white cardstock 9" wide x 6" high for a vertical-folded card size of 4½" wide x 6" high.
- Brayer sunflowers onto the background with a soft rubber brayer, then stamp additional sunflowers on top of the brayered ones.
- Stamp one twig frame, additional sunflowers, and four photo corners onto sticker paper and cut out.
- Place the twig frame sticker on the front of the card as shown, then place the sunflower stickers.
- Stamp three bees directly onto the cardstock, overlapping the brayered sunflowers. Make very small dots for the "bee trails" with an extrafine-tip black pigment marker.
- Open the card and place it on a cutting mat. Carefully cut out the inside of the twig frame, around the sunflowers as shown, with a sharp craft knife. This opening in the frame dictates the position of the color-copied photo to be placed on the inside of the card.

photo that is placed on the inside of the card.

Then, additional detailing on the front and on the inside can be stamped or embossed directly onto the cardstock or stamped or embossed onto sticker paper, cut out, and adhered to the cardstock.

In some instances, detailing may be desired on the back of the card. For example, a stamped or handwritten greeting, such as "Stamped Especially For You", along with a stamped image that coordinates with the theme of the card.

Stickers can also be used to add color and dimension. When adding stickers — preprinted or made from sticker paper — overlap as desired to add interest.

Because of the configuration of this type of frame card, there is limited space for writing on the inside of the card. The greeting can be handwritten directly onto the cardstock.

**Inside of
Sunflower Boy Card ➤**

- Crop the photo to fit the opening in the frame (window) and adhere it in place on the inside of the card with an appropriate adhesive.

- Place the stamped photo corner stickers at each corner, overlapping the photo as shown.

▲ Front of Sunflower Boy Card

- Showing the inside of the twig frame removed.

Fishing Friends Card

Shown at right and
on page 19.

- Shown smaller than actual size.
- Cut white cardstock 6" wide x 9" high for a horizontal-folded card size of 6" wide x 4¹/₂" high.
- Brayer trees onto the background with a soft rubber brayer, then stamp additional trees on top of the brayered ones.
- Stamp one wood frame, one tree, and four photo corners onto sticker paper and cut out.
- Place the wood frame sticker on the front of the card as shown, then place the tree sticker.
- Open the card and place it on a cutting mat. Carefully cut out the inside of the wood frame, around the tree as shown, with a sharp craft knife. This opening in the frame dictates the position of the color-copied photo to be placed on the inside of the card.

▲ Inside of Fishing Friends Card

- Crop the photo to fit the opening in the frame (window) and adhere it in place on the inside of the card with an appropriate adhesive.
- Draw a wiggly-lined box around the photo, ¹/₈" from all outside edges, with a green pigment marker. Place the stamped photo corner stickers at each corner, overlapping the photo as shown.

▲ Front of Fishing Friends Card

- Showing the inside of the wood frame removed.

Shown at left and below.

- Shown smaller than actual size.
- Cut white cardstock 6" wide x 9" high for a horizontal-folded card size of 6" wide x 4½" high.
- Brayer a watercolor effect onto the background with markers and a sponge brayer, then stamp marbles (for bubbles) directly onto the cardstock.
- Stamp one camera frame, three assorted seashells, and four photo corners onto sticker paper and cut out.
- Place the camera frame sticker on the front of the card as shown, then place the seashell stickers.
- Open the card and place it on a cutting mat. Carefully cut out the inside of the camera frame as shown with a sharp craft knife. This opening in the frame dictates the position of the color-copied photo to be placed on the inside of the card.

▲ Inside of Beach Baby Card

- Crop the photo to fit the opening in the frame (window) and adhere it in place on the inside of the card with an appropriate adhesive.
- Draw a wiggly-lined box around the photo, ⅛" from all outside edges, with an aqua blue pigment marker. Place the stamped photo corner stickers at each corner, overlapping the photo as shown.

▲ Front of Beach Baby Card

- Showing the inside of the camera frame removed.

Welcome Baby Card

Shown at left and
on page 19.

- Shown smaller than actual size.
- Cut white cardstock 6" wide x 9" high for a horizontal-folded card size of 6" wide x 4½" high.
- Sponge horizontal stripes onto the background with re-inkers and a compressed sponge.
- Stamp one ribbon frame with a bow and four photo corners onto sticker paper and cut out.
- Place the ribbon frame sticker on the front of the card as shown.
- Open the card and place it on a cutting mat. Carefully cut out the inside of the ribbon frame as shown with a sharp craft knife. This opening in the frame dictates the position of the color-copied photo to be placed on the inside of the card.

▲ Inside of Welcome Baby Card

- Crop the photo to fit the opening in the frame (window) and adhere it in place on the inside of the card with an appropriate adhesive.
- Place the stamped photo corner stickers at each corner, overlapping the photo as shown.

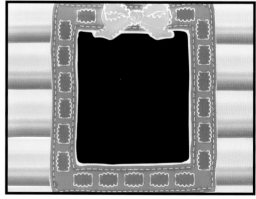

▲ Front of Welcome Baby Card

- Showing the inside of the ribbon frame removed.

Double-Window Photo Frame Cards

DOUBLE-WINDOW PHOTO FRAME CARDS

Shown on pages 25-28.

These photo frame cards can be made in any size and used both vertically and horizontally. The ones shown have been made from cardstock because it folds well and can withstand the weight of the stamped embellishments.

To begin, the size of the card must be determined. Once the cardstock has been cut and folded, any background can be applied over the cardstock on one or both sides as desired.

Because these are photo frame cards, frames are then stamped or embossed directly onto the cardstock or stamped or embossed onto sticker paper, cut out, and adhered to the cardstock. Once the insides of the frames have been cut out and removed, the frames (windows) will accentuate the photos that are placed on the inside of the card.

Then, additional detailing on the front and on the inside can be stamped or embossed directly onto the cardstock or stamped or embossed onto sticker paper, cut out, and adhered to the cardstock.

In some instances, detailing may be desired on the back of the card. For example, a stamped or handwritten greeting, such as "Stamped Espe-cially For You", along with a stamped image that coordinates with the theme of the card.

Stickers can also be used to add color and dimension. When adding stickers — preprinted or made from sticker paper — overlap as desired to add interest.

The greeting on the inside of the card can be stamped or handwritten directly onto the cardstock.

Strawberry Girl Card

Shown on pages 25-27.

- Shown smaller than actual size.
- Cut white coated cardstock 10½" wide x 8½" high for a vertical-folded card size of 5¼" wide x 8½" high.
- Repeatedly stamp a teal checkerboard pattern onto the background.
- Stamp two ribbon heart frames, one ribbon tag, and eighteen strawberries onto sticker paper and cut out.
- Place the ribbon heart frame stickers on the front of the card as shown, then place nine strawberry stickers.
- Open the card and place it on a cutting mat. Carefully cut out the insides of the ribbon heart frames as shown with a sharp craft knife. These openings in the frames dictate the position of the color-copied photos to be placed on the inside of the card.
- Crop the photos to fit the openings in the frames (windows) and adhere them to a teal bond paper or cardstock mat with an appropriate adhesive. Trim the mat to ⅛" as shown. Then, adhere the photos in place on the inside of the card.
- Stamp "Just for You!" inside the ribbon tag sticker.
- Place the ribbon tag and the remaining nine strawberry stickers, overlapping the photos as shown.

Inside of Strawberry Girl Card ►

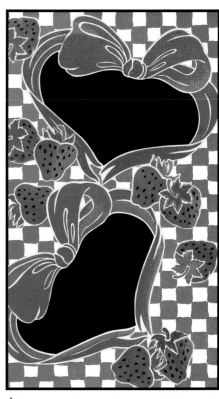

▲ Front of Strawberry Girl Card

- Showing the insides of the ribbon heart frames removed.

Bunches of Love Card

Shown below and
on page 25.

- Shown smaller than actual size.

- Cut white coated cardstock 10¹/₂" wide x 10¹/₄" high for a vertical-folded card size of 5¹/₄" wide x 10¹/₄" high.

- Draw double-vertical stripes onto the background with a fine-tip blue pigment marker.

- Stamp two lace frames, two bows, one ribbon tag, eight photo corners, one greeting, and five hearts onto sticker paper and cut out.

- Place the lace frame stickers on the front of the card as shown, then place the bow and heart stickers.

- Open the card and place it on a cutting mat. Carefully cut out the insides of the lace frames as shown with a sharp craft knife. These openings in the frames dictate the position of the color-copied photos to be placed on the inside of the card.

- Crop the photos to fit the openings in the frames (windows) and adhere them to a blue bond paper or cardstock mat with an appropriate adhesive. Trim the mat to ¹/₄" as shown. Then, adhere the photos in place on the inside of the card.

- Write a greeting inside the ribbon tag sticker with a blue pigment marker.

- Place the ribbon tag, stamped greeting, and photo corner stickers, over-lapping the photos as shown.

▲ Inside of
Bunches of Love Card

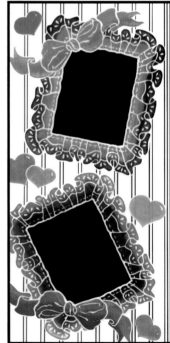

▲ Front of
Bunches of Love Card

- Showing the insides of the lace frames removed.

28

Triple-Window Photo Frame Cards

TRIPLE-WINDOW PHOTO FRAME CARDS

Shown on pages 29-33.

These photo frame cards can be made in any size and used both vertically and horizontally. The ones shown have been made from cardstock because it folds well and can withstand the weight of the stamped embellishments.

To begin, the size of the card must be determined. Once the cardstock has been cut and folded, any background can be applied over the cardstock on one or both sides as desired.

Because these are photo frame cards, frames are then stamped or embossed directly onto the cardstock or

Continued on page 32.

Cowboy Cuties Card

Shown above and on pages 29 & 31.

- Shown smaller than actual size.
- Cut ivory cardstock with a recycled fiber 11 1/2" wide x 14" high for a horizontal-folded card size of 11 1/2" wide x 7" high.

- No stamping or special techniques were used on this background.
- Stamp three rope frames, five cowboy hats, three lassos, several small stars, and twelve assorted photo corners onto sticker paper and cut out.
- Place the rope frame stickers on the front of the card as shown, then place the cowboy hat and star stickers.
- Write the word "Howdy" in-side one of the lasso stickers with a red pigment calligraphy marker, then place it as shown.
- Open the card and place it on a cutting mat. Carefully cut out the insides of the rope frames as shown with a sharp craft knife. These openings in the frames dictate the position of the color-copied photos to be placed on the inside of the card.

▲ Inside of Cowboy Cuties Card

- Crop the photos to fit the openings in the frames (windows) and adhere them in place on the inside of the card with an appropriate adhesive.

- Draw a wiggly-lined box around each photo, $1/8$" from all outside edges, with a black pigment marker. Place the stamped photo corner stickers at each corner, overlapping the photos as shown, then place the remaining lasso stickers.

- Write the words "To Grandma" and "From Joey" inside the lasso stickers with the same black pigment marker.

◄ Front of Cowboy Cuties Card

- Showing the insides of the rope frames removed.

Continued from page 30.

stamped or embossed onto sticker paper, cut out, and adhered to the cardstock. Once the insides of the frames have been cut out and removed, the frames (windows) will accentuate the photos that are placed on the inside of the card.

Then, additional detailing on the front and on the inside can be stamped or embossed directly onto the cardstock or stamped or embossed onto sticker paper, cut out, and adhered to the cardstock.

In some instances, detailing may be desired on the back of the card. For example, a stamped or handwritten greeting, such as "Stamped Especially For You", along with a stamped image that coordinates with the theme of the card.

Stickers can also be used to add color and dimension. When adding stickers — preprinted or made from sticker paper — overlap as desired to add interest.

The greeting on the inside of the card can be handwritten directly onto the cardstock.

Splish Splash Card

Shown above and on pages 29 & 33.

- Shown smaller than actual size.
- Cut white cardstock $8^1/_4$" wide x $16^1/_2$" high for a horizontal-folded card size of $8^1/_4$" square.
- Sponge wavy stripes onto the background with re-inkers and a compressed sponge.
- Stamp three porthole frames, seven assorted tropical fish, and five beach balls onto sticker paper and cut out.

- Place the porthole frame stickers on the front of the card as shown, then place the tropical fish stickers.
- Open the card and place it on a cutting mat. Carefully cut out the insides of the porthole frames as shown with a sharp craft knife. These openings in the frames dictate the position of the color-copied photos to be placed on the inside of the card.

◄ Inside of
Splish Splash Card

• Crop the photos to fit the openings in the frames (windows) and adhere them in place on the inside of the card with an appropriate adhesive.

• Place the beach ball stickers as shown.

Front of
Splish Splash Card ➤

• Showing the insides of the porthole frames removed.

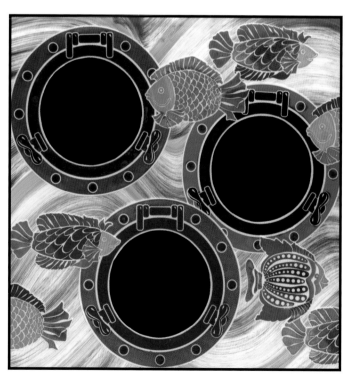

Photo Frame Envelopes

PHOTO FRAME ENVELOPES

Shown on pages 34-39.

These photo frame envelopes can be made from any size envelope, but all those shown measure 6½" wide x 4¾" high (not including flap) which is known commercially as an A6 envelope.

To begin, any background can be applied over a coated (glossy) envelope on one or both sides as desired.

Because these are photo frame envelopes, a frame is then stamped or embossed onto sticker paper and cut out. Once the inside of the frame has been cut out and removed, the frame will accentuate the photo that is placed behind it.

Then, additional detailing can be stamped or embossed bossed directly onto the envelope or stamped or embossed onto sticker paper, cut out, and adhered to the envelope.

Stickers can also be used to add color and dimension. When adding stickers — preprinted or made from sticker paper — overlap as desired to add interest.

When designing photo frame envelopes, make certain to leave enough space to address the envelope large enough to be easily read.

Little League Envelope

Shown above and on page 34.

- Shown smaller than actual size.
- Repeatedly stamp a single-color newspaper-print onto the front of a white coated A6 envelope.
- Stamp one trophy frame onto sticker paper and cut out. Draw four various-sized word boxes onto sticker paper with a brown pigment marker and cut out.
- Place the trophy frame sticker on a cutting mat. Carefully cut out the inside of the trophy frame as shown with a sharp craft knife. This opening in the frame dictates the position of the color-copied photo to be placed behind it.
- Crop the photo to fit the opening in the frame and adhere it in place on the back of the sticker.
- Place the trophy frame sticker on the front of the envelope as shown, then place the word box stickers.
- Write the name of the addressee and the address inside the word boxes as shown with a brown pigment marker. Write the word "Champs" at the bottom of the trophy frame with a brown pigment calligraphy marker. Shadow the trophy frame and the word boxes with a brown pigment marker.
- Finally, add a postage stamp.

State Champs Envelope

Shown above and on page 34.

- Shown actual size.
- Brayer a rainbow effect onto the front of a white coated A6 envelope with a rainbow pad and black foam brayer. Lightly mist the brayer with water to create the watercolor effect.
- Stamp one newspaper frame and eight basketballs onto sticker paper and cut out.

- Place the newspaper frame sticker on a cutting mat. Carefully cut out the inside of the newspaper frame as shown with a sharp craft knife. This opening in the frame dictates the position of the color-copied photo to be placed behind it.
- Crop the photo to fit the opening in the frame and adhere it in place on the back of the sticker.
- Place the newspaper frame sticker on the front of the envelope as shown, then place the basketball stickers. Trim the basketballs as nec-

essary at the edges of the envelope.
- Write the name of the addressee and the address near the bottom of the envelope as shown with a black pigment marker.
- Draw dotted lines between the basketballs to create the illusion of movement.
- Write the words "State Champs" for the headline of the newspaper with green and blue pigment markers.
- Finally, add a postage stamp.

I Love Santa Envelope

Shown below and on page 34.

- Shown actual size.
- Repeatedly stamp a black checkerboard pattern onto the front of a white coated A6 envelope.
- Stamp one ribbon heart frame, one ribbon tag, and one small wrapped gift box onto sticker paper and cut out.
- Place the ribbon heart frame sticker on a cutting mat. Carefully cut out the inside of the ribbon heart frame as shown with a sharp craft knife. This opening in the frame dictates the position of the color-copied photo to be placed behind it.
- Crop the photo to fit the opening in the frame and adhere it in place on the back of the sticker.
- Place the ribbon heart frame sticker on the front of the envelope as shown, then place the ribbon tag and small wrapped gift box stickers.
- Write the name of the addressee and the address inside the ribbon tag as shown with a black pigment marker.
- Finally, add a postage stamp on top of the small wrapped gift box sticker.

First Birthday Envelope

Shown below and
on page 34.

- Shown actual size.
- Repeatedly stamp colorful balloons and confetti onto the front of a white coated A6 envelope.
- Stamp one birthday cake frame with a single birthday candle onto sticker paper and cut out.
- Place the birthday cake frame sticker on a cutting mat. Carefully cut out the inside of the birthday cake frame as shown with a sharp craft knife. This opening in the frame dictates the position of the color-copied photo to be placed behind it.
- Crop the photo to fit the opening in the frame and adhere it in place on the back of the sticker.
- Place the birthday cake frame sticker on the front of the envelope as shown.
- Write the name of the addressee and the address to the right of the birthday cake frame as shown with colored pigment markers.
- Finally, add a postage stamp.

Back-To-School Envelope

Shown above and on page 34.

- Shown actual size.
- No stamping or special techniques were used on this white coated A6 envelope.
- Stamp one adobe frame and eight pencils onto sticker paper and cut out.

- Place the adobe frame sticker on a cutting mat. Carefully cut out the inside of the adobe frame as shown with a sharp craft knife. This opening in the frame dictates the position of the color-copied photo to be placed behind it.
- Crop the photo to fit the opening in the frame and adhere it in place on the back of the sticker.

- Place the adobe frame sticker on the front of the envelope as shown, then place the pencil stickers. Trim the pencils as necessary at the edges of the envelope.
- Write the name of the addressee and the address around two of the outside edges of the adobe frame as shown with a blue pigment marker.
- Finally, add a postage stamp.

Fancy Floral Envelopes

FANCY FLORAL ENVELOPES

Shown on pages 40-43.

These fancy floral envelopes can be made from any size envelope, but all those shown measure 6$\frac{1}{2}$" wide x 4$\frac{3}{4}$" high (not including flap) which is known commercially as an A6 envelope.

To begin, any background can be applied over a coated (glossy) envelope on one or both sides as desired.

Next, a compressed sponge background is applied onto sticker paper. When the ink is completely dry, an open vase (or fishbowl) is stamped onto the sticker paper directly over the compressed sponge background. It should then be cut out along the stamped outline of the vase — do not leave a border around the vase.

Flowers and greenery are stamped onto sticker paper and cut out.

Continued on page 42.

Wildflower Envelope

Shown above and on page 40.

- Shown smaller than actual size.
- Brayer a rainbow effect onto the front of a white coated A6 envelope with a rainbow pad and black foam brayer. Lightly mist the brayer with water to create the watercolor effect.
- Sponge diagonal stripes onto sticker paper with re-inkers and a compressed sponge to create the background for the vase.
- Stamp the fishbowl (vase) directly over the compressed sponge background and cut out, leaving no border.
- Stamp the flowers and greenery onto sticker paper and cut out.
- Arrange the vase of flowers and greenery and place it on the front of the envelope as shown.
- Write the name of the addressee and the address to the right of the vase of flowers with colored pigment markers.
- Finally, add a postage stamp.

Continued from page 41.

If desired, additional detailing, such as tiny accent flowers and greenery, can be stamped or embossed directly onto the envelope or stamped or embossed onto sticker paper, cut out, and adhered to the envelope.

Stickers can also be used to add color and dimension. When adding stickers — preprinted or made from sticker paper — overlap as desired to add interest.

To arrange the bouquet of flowers in the vase, tack the bottom

Tulip Envelope

Shown above and on page 40.

- Shown smaller than actual size.
- Brayer a rainbow effect onto the front of a white coated A6 envelope with a rainbow pad and black foam brayer. Lightly mist the brayer with water to create the watercolor effect.

- Stamp tiny accent flowers and greenery directly onto the envelope over the watercolor background, positioned to be behind the vase of flowers.
- Sponge wavy stripes onto sticker paper with re-inkers and a compressed sponge to create the background for the vase.
- Stamp the vase directly over the compressed sponge background and cut out, leaving no border.

- Stamp the flowers and greenery onto sticker paper and cut out.
- Arrange the vase of flowers and greenery (over the tiny accent flowers and greenery) and place it on the front of the envelope as shown.
- Write the name of the addressee and the address to the right of the vase of flowers with colored pigment markers.
- Finally, add a postage stamp.

of the stamped vase in position on the envelope and place the flowers and greenery in and around the vase as desired, overlapping to add dimension. When the bouquet is in place, permanently adhere each piece in position.

When designing fancy floral envelopes, make certain to leave enough space to address the envelope large enough to be easily read.

Forget-Me-Not Envelope

Shown above and on page 40.

- Shown smaller than actual size.
- Brayer a rainbow effect onto the front of a white coated A6 envelope with a rainbow pad and black foam brayer. Lightly mist the brayer with water to create the watercolor effect.
- Stamp accent greenery directly onto the envelope over the watercolor background, positioned to be behind the vase of flowers.
- Sponge diagonal stripes in opposite directions onto sticker paper with re-inkers and a compressed sponge to create the plaid background for the vase.
- Stamp the fishbowl (vase) directly over the compressed sponge background and cut out, leaving no border.
- Stamp the flowers and greenery onto sticker paper and cut out.
- Arrange the vase of flowers and greenery (over the accent greenery) and place it on the front of the envelope as shown.
- Write the name of the addressee and the address to the right of the vase of flowers with colored pigment markers.
- Finally, add a postage stamp.

Oversized Envelopes

OVERSIZED ENVELOPES

Shown on pages 44-47.

These oversized envelopes measure 12½" wide x 9½" high (not including flap).

To begin, any background can be applied over a coated (glossy) envelope on one or both sides as desired.

Then, additional detailing on the front can be stamped or embossed directly onto the envelope or stamped or embossed onto sticker paper, cut out, and adhered to the envelope.

Stickers can also be used to add color and dimension. When adding stickers — preprinted or made from sticker paper — overlap as desired to add interest.

When addressing oversized envelopes, make certain to stamp or write the name of the addressee and the address big, bold, and beautiful!

Radiant Roses Envelope

Shown above and on page 44.

- Shown smaller than actual size.

- Brayer a watercolor effect onto the front of a white coated oversized envelope with markers and a sponge brayer.
- Stamp several rose clusters and splatters directly onto the envelope over the watercolor background.

- Write the name of the addressee and the address on the envelope as shown with colored pigment calligraphy markers.
- Finally, add a postage stamp. Postage may vary depending upon the size of the envelope.

Sensational Sunflower Envelope

Shown below and on page 44.

- Shown smaller than actual size.

- Brayer sunflowers onto the front of a white coated over-sized envelope with a soft rubber brayer, then stamp additional sunflowers on top of the brayered ones.

- Stamp forget-me-nots directly onto the envelope over the brayered background.

- Spatter the brayered background with a twisting spatter brush.

- Write the name of the addressee and the address on the envelope as shown with colored pigment calligraphy markers.

- Finally, add a postage stamp. Postage may vary depending upon the size of the envelope.

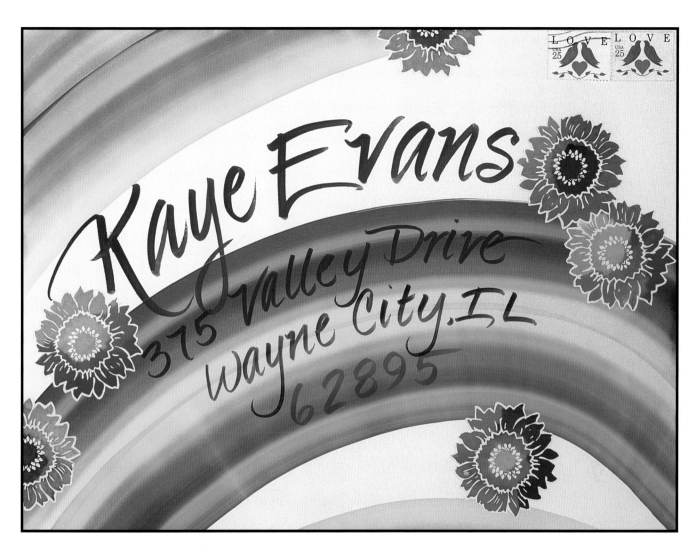

L O V E
USA
25

L O V E
USA
25

Kaye Evans
375 Valley Drive
Wayne City, IL
62895

Rainbow of Colors Envelope

Shown above and on page 44.

- Shown smaller than actual size.

- Sponge curved stripes onto the front of a white coated oversized envelope with re-inkers and a compressed sponge to create a rainbow.

- Stamp six sunflowers onto sticker paper and cut out.

- Place the sunflower stickers on the front of the envelope as shown. Trim the sunflowers as necessary at the edges of the envelope.

- Write the name of the addressee and the address on the envelope as shown with colored pigment calligraphy markers.

- Finally, add a postage stamp. Postage may vary depending upon the size of the envelope.

Photo Frame Wooden Postcards

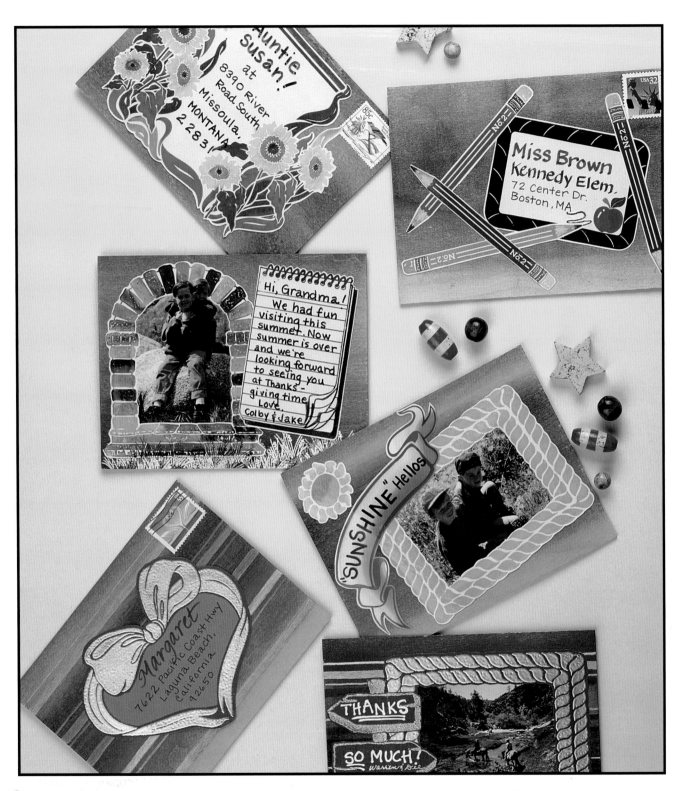

Continued from page 49.

stamped or embossed onto sticker paper, cut out, and adhered to the front and back of the postcard.

Stickers can also be used to add color and dimension. When adding stickers — preprinted or made from sticker paper — overlap as desired to add interest.

When designing photo frame postcards, make certain to leave enough space on the front of the postcard to address it large enough to be easily read.

The greeting on the back of the postcard can be handwritten directly onto the plywood or handwritten on sticker paper, cut out, and adhered to the postcard.

These postcards should be delivered to any postal service facility for hand-canceling.

▼ Front of Thanks, Teacher Wooden Postcard

- Stamp one chalkboard frame and four pencils onto sticker paper and cut out.
- Place the chalkboard frame sticker on the front of the postcard as shown, then place the pencil stickers.

- Write the name of the addressee and the address inside the chalkboard frame with colored pigment markers.

- Finally, add a postage stamp. Postage may vary depending upon the size of the postcard.
- Make certain the postal service hand-cancels the postcard.

50

PHOTO FRAME WOODEN POSTCARDS

Shown on pages 48-58.

These photo frame wooden postcards can be made in any size, but all those shown measure 6¼" wide x 4¾" high. They have been made from ⅛" birch plywood because it is an extremely durable, yet incredibly lightweight wood, making it the ideal choice when making postcards that will be sent via the postal service.

To begin, the size of the postcard must be determined. Once the plywood has been cut, any background can be applied over the plywood on one or both sides as desired.

Because these are photo frame postcards, a frame is then stamped or embossed onto sticker paper and cut out. Once the inside of the frame has been cut out and removed, the frame will accentuate the photo that is placed behind it.

Then, additional detailing can be stamped or embossed directly onto the plywood or

Continued on page 50.

Thanks, Teacher Wooden Postcard

Shown at right and on pages 48 & 50.

- Shown smaller than actual size.
- Brayer a rainbow effect onto the back and front of a wooden postcard with a rainbow pad and black foam brayer.
- Stamp one rope frame, one banner, and two apples onto sticker paper and cut out.
- Place the rope frame sticker on a cutting mat. Carefully cut out the inside of the rope frame as shown with a sharp craft knife. This opening in the sticker dictates the position of the color-copied photo to be placed behind it.

▼ Back of Thanks, Teacher Wooden Postcard

- Crop the photo to fit the opening in the frame and adhere it in place on the back of the sticker.
- Place the rope frame sticker on the back of the postcard as shown, then place the banner and apple stickers.
- Write the words "Thanks, Teacher" inside the banner with a red pigment marker.

49

"Sunshine" Hellos Wooden Postcard

Shown at right and on page 48.

- Shown smaller than actual size.
- Brayer a rainbow effect onto the back and front of a wooden postcard with a rainbow pad and black foam brayer.
- Stamp one rope frame, one banner, and one sun onto sticker paper and cut out.
- Place the rope frame sticker on a cutting mat. Carefully cut out the inside of the rope frame as shown with a sharp craft knife. This opening in the sticker dictates the position of the color-copied photo to be placed behind it.
- Crop the photo to fit the opening in the frame and adhere it in place on the back of the sticker.
- Place the rope frame sticker on the back of the postcard as shown, then place the banner and sun stickers.
- Write the words "Sunshine Hellos" inside the banner with a black pigment marker.
- Stamp one camera frame onto sticker paper and cut out.
- Place the camera frame sticker on the front of the postcard as shown.

▲ Back of Sunshine Hellos Wooden Postcard
▼ Front of Sunshine Hellos Wooden Postcard

- Write the name of the addressee and the address inside the camera frame with colored pigment markers.
- Finally, add a postage stamp. Postage may vary depending upon the size of the postcard.
- Make certain the postal service hand-cancels the postcard.

▲ Back of Summer Fun Wooden Postcard

Summer Fun Wooden Postcard

Shown above and on pages 48 & 53.

- Shown actual size.
- Brayer a rainbow effect onto the back and front of a wooden postcard with a rainbow pad and black foam brayer.
- Emboss the grass directly onto the back with white and gold embossing powders.

- Stamp one brick archway frame and one notebook onto sticker paper and cut out.
- Stamp additional grass at the bottom of the brick archway frame.
- Place the brick archway frame sticker on a cutting mat. Carefully cut out the inside of the brick archway frame as shown with a sharp craft knife. This opening in the sticker dictates the position of the color-copied photo to be placed behind it.

- Crop the photo to fit the opening in the frame and adhere it in place on the back of the sticker. In this instance, the photo was cropped so the boys' heads come out and over the upper part of the brick archway frame.
- Place the brick archway frame sticker on the back of the postcard as shown, then place the notebook sticker.
- Write the greeting on the lines of the notebook with a brown pigment marker.

- Emboss the small leaves directly onto the front with white embossing powder, positioned to be behind the twig frame.
- Stamp one twig frame onto sticker paper and cut out.

- Place the twig frame sticker on the front of the postcard over the small white embossed leaves as shown.
- Write the name of the addressee and the address inside the twig frame with green pigment markers.

- Finally, add a postage stamp. Postage may vary depending upon the size of the postcard.
- Make certain the postal service hand-cancels the postcard.

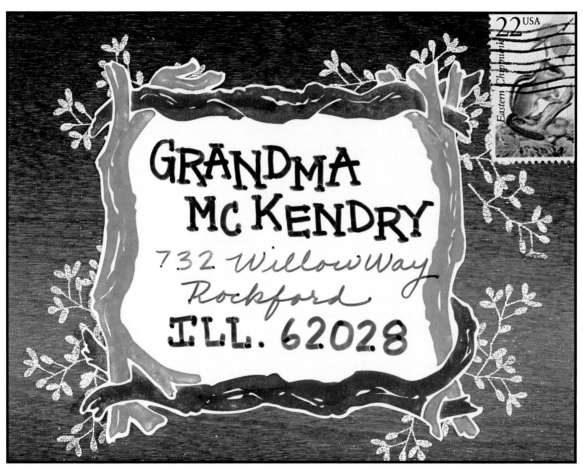

▲ Front of Summer Fun Wooden Postcard

▲ Back of Be My Valentine Wooden Postcard

Be My Valentine Wooden Postcard

Shown above and
on pages 48 & 55.

- Shown actual size.
- Brayer a rainbow effect onto the back and front of a wooden postcard with a rainbow pad and black foam brayer.
- Horizontally separate the different colors of the rainbow pad on the back and front with gold and silver metallic markers.
- Emboss one ribbon heart frame onto hot pink cardstock with silver embossing powder and cut out. Emboss one ribbon tag onto bright yellow cardstock with silver embossing powder and cut out.
- Place the ribbon heart frame on a cutting mat. Carefully cut out the inside of the ribbon heart frame as shown with a sharp craft knife. This opening in the frame dictates the position of the color-copied photo to be placed behind it.
- Crop the photo to fit the opening in the frame and adhere it in place on the back with an appropriate adhesive.
- Place the ribbon heart frame on the back of the postcard as shown, then place the ribbon tag. Adhere them in place with an appropriate adhesive.
- Write the words "Be My Valentine" and the sender's name inside the ribbon tag with blue and red pigment markers.

54

▲ Front of Be My Valentine Wooden Postcard

- Emboss one ribbon heart frame onto dark green cardstock with silver embossing powder and cut out.

- Place the ribbon heart frame on a cutting mat. Carefully cut out the inside of the ribbon heart frame as shown with a sharp craft knife. This opening in the frame dictates the position of the hot pink cardstock to be placed behind it.

- Crop the hot pink cardstock to fit the opening in the frame and adhere it in place on the back with an appropriate adhesive.

- Place the ribbon heart frame on the front of the postcard as shown and adhere it in place with an appropriate adhesive.

- Write the name of the addressee and the address inside the ribbon heart frame with black pigment markers.

- Finally, add a postage stamp. Postage may vary depending upon the size of the postcard.

- Make certain the postal service hand-cancels the postcard.

Rankin Ranch Wooden Postcard

Shown below and on pages 48 & 57.

- Shown actual size.
- Brayer a rainbow effect onto the back and front of a wooden postcard with a rainbow pad and black foam brayer. Brayer the back horizontally and the front vertically.
- Horizontally separate the different colors of the rainbow pad on the back and vertically on the front with gold and silver metallic markers.
- Emboss one rope frame onto dark green cardstock with silver embossing powder and cut out. Emboss one directional sign onto dark plum cardstock with bronze embossing powder and cut out.
- Place the rope frame on a cutting mat. Carefully cut out the inside of the rope frame as shown with a sharp craft knife. This opening in the frame dictates the position of the color-copied photo to be placed behind it.
- Crop the photo to fit the opening in the frame and adhere it in place on the back with an appropriate adhesive.
- Place the rope frame on the back of the postcard as shown, then place the directional sign. Adhere them in place with an appropriate adhesive.
- Write the words "Thanks So Much!" and the senders' names inside the directional sign with metallic markers.

▲ Back of Rankin Ranch Wooden Postcard

▲ Front of Rankin Ranch Wooden Postcard

- Emboss one rope frame onto navy blue cardstock with silver embossing powder and cut out. Emboss one bandana onto dark green cardstock with gold and bronze embossing powders and cut out.
- Place the rope frame on the front of the postcard as shown, then place the bandana. Adhere them in place with an appropriate adhesive.
- Write the name of the addressee and the address inside the rope frame with a metallic marker.
- Finally, add a postage stamp. Postage may vary depending upon the size of the postcard.
- Make certain the postal service hand-cancels the postcard.

Sunflower Smiles Wooden Postcard

Shown at right and on page 48.

- Shown smaller than actual size.
- Brayer a rainbow effect onto the back and front of a wooden postcard with a rainbow pad and black foam brayer.
- Stamp one wood frame, one scroll, and three sunflowers with stems onto sticker paper and cut out.
- Place the wood frame sticker on a cutting mat. Carefully cut out the inside of the wood frame as shown with a sharp craft knife. This opening in the sticker dictates the position of the color-copied photo to be placed behind it.
- Crop the photo to fit the opening in the frame and adhere it in place on the back of the sticker.
- Place the wood frame sticker on the back of the postcard as shown, then place the scroll and sunflower stickers.
- Write the greeting inside the scroll with a brown pigment marker.
- Stamp one twisting leaf frame and several sunflowers with stems onto sticker paper and cut out.
- Place the twisting leaf frame sticker on the front of the postcard as

▲ Back of Sunflower Smiles Wooden Postcard
▼ Front of Sunflower Smiles Wooden Postcard

shown, then place the sunflower stickers.
- Write the name of the addressee and the address inside the twisting leaf frame with brown pigment markers.

- Finally, add a postage stamp. Postage may vary depending upon the size of the postcard.
- Make certain the postal service hand-cancels the postcard.

Address Labels

ADDRESS LABELS

Shown on pages 59-61.

These labels can be made in any size, but all those shown are frame stamps that have been used to create decorative address labels.

The frames have been stamped onto sticker paper and cut out. Because of the adhesive backing on the sticker paper, labels can be created instantly.

To begin, stamp any frame onto sticker paper and cut out.

If desired, any background that will contrast or coordinate with the label can be applied over a coated (glossy) envelope or package before the label is adhered.

Birthday Label

Shown above and on page 59.

- Shown actual size.
- Stamp one birthday cake frame with five birthday candles onto sticker paper and cut out.
- Place the birthday cake frame sticker (label) on the front of an envelope as shown. The white coated A6 envelope shown has a compressed sponge background that was designed to coordinate with the colors of the label.
- Write the name of the addressee and the address inside the birthday cake frame with colored pigment calligraphy markers.
- Finally, add a postage stamp.

60

Tulip Label

Shown at left and on page 59.

- Shown smaller than actual size.
- Stamp one twisting tulip frame onto sticker paper and cut out.
- Place the twisting tulip frame sticker (label) on the front of an envelope as shown. The white coated A6 envelope shown has a stamped checkerboard pattern background that was designed to contrast with the colors of the label.
- Write the name of the addressee and the address inside the twisting tulip frame with a blue pigment marker.
- Finally, add a postage stamp.

Southwestern Label

Shown at right and on page 59.

- Shown smaller than actual size.
- Stamp one brick archway frame frame and a variety of cacti onto sticker paper and cut out.
- Place the brick archway frame sticker (label) on the front of an envelope as shown. The white coated A6 envelope shown has a sponge-brayered watercolor background that was designed to coordinate with the colors of the label. The bricks and rocks were stamped directly onto the envelope over the background, positioned around and behind the brick archway frame as shown.
- Place the cacti stickers as shown.

- Write the name of the addressee and the address inside the brick archway frame with a brown pigment marker.

- Finally, add a postage stamp.

Photo Frame Calendars

PHOTO FRAME
CALENDARS
Shown on pages 62-71.

These photo frame calendars can be made in any size, but all those shown measure 5" wide x 7" high. They have been made from coated (glossy) cardstock because cardstock can withstand the weight of the stamped embellishments.

To begin, the size of the calendar must be determined. Once the cardstock has been cut, any background can be applied over the cardstock.

The name of the calendar month and the days of the month can be stamped directly onto the cardstock, printed onto the cardstock with a computer laser printer, or calendar pages can be purchased with this information preprinted.

Because these are photo frame calendars, frames are then stamped or embossed onto sticker paper and cut out. Once the insides of the frames have been cut out and removed, the frames will accentuate the photos that are placed behind them.

Using photo corner stickers is an alternative to framing the photos. When using photo corners, a mat behind the photo is recommended and adds dimension to the photo frame calendar.

January
Shown above.

- Shown smaller than actual size.
- Draw diagonal stripes onto the background of white coated cardstock (preprinted with the calendar month information) with a fine-tip red pigment marker.
- Stamp two different rose corners (for photo corners) onto sticker paper and cut out.
- Crop the photo as desired and adhere it to a red bond paper or cardstock mat with an appropriate adhesive. Trim the mat to $1/8$" as shown with deckle-edged scissors.
- Place the matted photo on the calendar as shown and adhere it in place with an appropriate adhesive, then place the rose photo corner stickers at opposite corners, overlapping the photo as shown.

February

Shown at right.

- Shown actual size.
- Brayer ivy leaves onto the the background of white coated cardstock (pre-printed with the calendar month information) with a soft rubber brayer, then stamp additional ivy leaves on top of the brayered ones.
- Stamp small flowers on top of the ivy leaves as shown.
- Spatter green ink onto the background with a twisting spatter brush.
- Stamp one ribbon heart frame and additional ivy leaves onto sticker paper and cut out.
- Place the ribbon heart frame sticker on a cutting mat. Carefully cut out the inside of the ribbon heart frame as shown with a sharp craft knife. This opening in the sticker dictates the position of the color-copied photo to be placed behind it.
- Crop the photo to fit the opening in the frame and adhere it in place on the back of the sticker.
- Place the ribbon heart frame sticker on the calendar as shown, then place the ivy leaf stickers.

March

Shown above and on page 62.

- Shown smaller than actual size.
- Draw ticking stripes onto the background of white coated cardstock (preprinted with the calendar month information) with a fine-tip blue pigment marker.
- Stamp two bandanas (for photo corners) and several stars onto sticker paper and cut out.
- Crop the photo as desired and adhere it to a red bond paper or cardstock mat with an appropriate adhesive. Trim the mat to $1/8$" as shown.
- Place the matted photo on the calendar as shown and adhere it in place with an appropriate adhesive, then place the bandana photo corner stickers at opposite corners, overlapping the photo as shown.
- Place the star stickers on the calendar, overlapping the photo as shown. Trim the stars as necessary at the edges of the calendar.

April

Shown above and on page 62.

- Shown smaller than actual size.
- Streak ink diagonally across the background of white coated cardstock (preprinted with the calendar month information) with the brushstroke stamp to create the blue sky, then stamp raindrops on top of the streaked background.
- Stamp several clouds, three photo corners, and one umbrella (for fourth photo corner) onto sticker paper and cut out.
- Place the cloud stickers on the calendar as shown. Trim the clouds as necessary at the edges of the calendar.
- Crop the photo as desired and adhere it to a blue bond paper or cardstock mat with an appropriate adhesive. Trim the mat to $1/8$" as shown.
- Place the matted photo on the calendar as shown and adhere it in place with an appropriate adhesive, then place the umbrella and stamped photo corner stickers at each corner, overlapping the photo as shown.

May

Shown at left.

- Shown actual size.
- Stamp forget-me-not flowers onto the background of white coated cardstock (preprinted with the calendar month information), around the outside edges, to create a border.
- Stamp accent dots around the floral border as shown.
- Stamp one heart locket frame and two doves onto sticker paper and cut out.
- Place the heart locket frame sticker on a cutting mat. Carefully cut out the insides of the heart locket frame (both sides) as shown with a sharp craft knife. These openings in the sticker dictate the position of the color-copied photos to be placed behind them.
- Crop the photos to fit the openings in the frame and adhere them in place on the back of the sticker.
- Place the heart locket frame sticker on the calendar as shown, then place the dove stickers.

June

Shown above.

- Shown smaller than actual size.
- Sponge diagonal stripes onto the background of white coated cardstock (preprinted with the calendar month information) with re-inkers and a compressed sponge.
- Stamp one baby block frame onto sticker paper and cut out.
- Place the baby block frame sticker on a cutting mat. Carefully cut out the inside of the top of the middle baby block as shown with a sharp craft knife. This opening in the sticker dictates the position of the color-copied photo to be placed behind it.
- Crop the photo to fit the opening in the frame (middle baby block) and adhere it in place on the back of the sticker.
- Place the baby block frame sticker on the calendar as shown.

- Shown smaller than actual size.
- Brayer a watercolor effect onto the background of white coated cardstock (preprinted with the calendar month information) with markers and a sponge brayer. Use blue on the upper portion and yellow on the lower portion.
- Stamp clouds, sand, and wild grass directly onto the cardstock over the watercolor background to create the scene.
- Stamp one airplane frame, one sun, one sand-castle, and several assorted seashells onto sticker paper and cut out.
- Place the airplane frame sticker on a cutting mat. Carefully cut out the inside of the airplane frame as shown with a sharp craft knife. This opening in the sticker dictates the position of the color-copied photo to be placed behind it.
- Crop the photo to fit the opening in the frame and adhere it in place on the back of the sticker.
- Place the airplane frame sticker on the calendar as shown, then place the sun, sandcastle, and seashell stickers, overlapping the photo as shown.

August

Shown at right and
on page 62.

- Shown actual size.
- Brayer a watercolor effect onto the background of white coated cardstock (preprinted with the calendar month information) with markers and a sponge brayer to create the land-scape.
- Stamp clouds, hilltops, and wild grass directly onto the brayered background to create the scene.
- Sponge an airbrush effect onto the brayered and stamped background with markers and a wedge sponge to create the sky.
- Stamp one sun, one tree, and three butterflies directly onto the cardstock over the background. Make very small dots for the "butterfly trails", with an extrafine-tip black pigment marker.
- Stamp one tent frame and several small clusters of flowers onto sticker paper and cut out.
- Place the tent frame sticker on a cutting mat. Carefully cut out the inside of the tent frame as shown with a sharp craft knife. This opening in the sticker dictates the position of the color-copied photo to be placed behind it.
- Crop the photo to fit the opening in the frame and adhere it in place on the back of the sticker.

- Place the tent frame sticker on the calendar as shown, then place the flower stickers, overlapping the photo as shown.

68

September

Shown above and on page 62.

- Shown smaller than actual size.
- Draw double-vertical stripes onto the background of white coated cardstock (preprinted with the calendar month information) with a fine-tip teal pigment marker.
- Stamp one megaphone frame and several footballs onto sticker paper and cut out.
- Place the megaphone frame sticker on a cutting mat. Carefully cut out the inside of the megaphone frame as shown with a sharp craft knife. This opening in the sticker dictates the position of the color-copied photo to be placed behind it.
- Crop the photo to fit the opening in the frame and adhere it in place on the back of the sticker.
- Place the megaphone frame sticker on the calendar as shown, then place the football stickers.

October

Shown above.

- Shown smaller than actual size.
- Sponge stripes in horizontal and vertical directions onto the background of white coated cardstock (preprinted with the calendar month information) with re-inkers and a compressed sponge to create a plaid background.
- Stamp one camera frame, five bats, and five candy corn onto sticker paper and cut out.
- Place the camera frame sticker on a cutting mat. Carefully cut out the inside of the camera frame as shown with a sharp craft knife. This opening in the sticker dictates the position of the color-copied photo to be placed behind it.
- Crop the photo to fit the opening in the frame and adhere it in place on the back of the sticker.
- Place the camera frame sticker on the calendar as shown, then place the bat and candy corn stickers.

November

Shown at left.

- Shown actual size.
- Brayer stripes in opposite diagonal directions onto the background of white coated cardstock (preprinted with the calendar month information) with a soft rubber brayer to create a plaid background.
- Stamp one rope frame, two haystacks, and several assorted autumn leaves onto sticker paper and cut out.
- Place the rope frame sticker on a cutting mat. Carefully cut out the inside of the rope frame as shown with a sharp craft knife. This opening in the sticker dictates the position of the color-copied photo to be placed behind it.
- Crop the photo to fit the opening in the frame and adhere it in place on the back of the sticker.
- Place the rope frame sticker on the calendar as shown, then place the haystack and autumn leaf stickers, overlapping the photo as shown.

December

Shown at right.

- Shown actual size.
- Stamp a border of trees directly onto the background of white coated cardstock (preprinted with the calendar month information) across the upper portion to create the scene.
- Stamp accent dots above the border of trees as shown.
- Sponge an airbrush effect onto the stamped background with markers and a wedge sponge to create the sky.
- Add accent dots on top of the trees with the tip of a white ballpoint correction pen as shown.
- Stamp snow onto the background and cut a reverse paper mask in the snow shape to mask the white area above the snow. Place the mask in position and sponge an airbrush effect to shade the snow.
- Stamp one family auto frame and three birds onto sticker paper and cut out.
- Place the family auto frame sticker on a cutting mat. Carefully cut out the inside of the family auto frame as shown (leaving rear-view mirror) with a sharp craft knife. This opening in the sticker dictates the position of the color-copied photo to be placed behind it.
- Crop the photo to fit the opening in the frame and adhere it in place on the back of the sticker.

- Place the family auto frame sticker on the calendar as shown, then place the bird stickers.

- Write the words "Ho-Ho-Ho" inside the license plate frame with a fine-tip blue pigment marker.

Gift Bag and Tissue Paper

GIFT BAGS

Shown on page 72.

These gift bags can be made from any size bag, but the one shown measures 7³/₄" wide x 9³/₄" high.

To begin, any background can be applied over the gift bag on one or both sides as desired.

Then, additional detailing can be stamped or embossed directly onto the gift bag or stamped or embossed onto sticker paper, cut out, and adhered to the gift bag.

TISSUE PAPER

Shown on page 72.

Tissue paper, which comes in virtually any color, can be embellished with simple stamped images.

The tissue paper should be placed on a flat, padded surface.

To begin, any image can be stamped onto the tissue paper as desired.

Then, additional detailing can be stamped directly onto the tissue paper. For this application, embossing is not recommended and the use of sticker paper would make the tissue paper too heavy.

Western Gift Bag

Shown on page 72.

- No stamping or special techniques were used on the background of this gift bag.
- Stamp one banner onto sticker paper and cut out.
- Write the words "To: Colby!" inside the banner with blue and red pigment markers.
- Crop the photo as desired. Trim the photo with deckle-edged scissors.
- Adhere the photo to a navy blue bond paper or cardstock mat with an appropriate adhesive. Trim the mat to ¹/₄" as shown with deckle-edged scissors.

- Adhere the navy blue mat to a dark red bond paper or cardstock mat with an appropriate adhesive. Trim the mat to ¹/₂" as shown with deckle-edged scissors. Make certain the matted photo will fit on the front of the gift bag.
- Place the matted photo on the gift bag as shown and adhere it in place with an appropriate adhesive.
- Place the banner sticker at the bottom of the photo as shown.

Western Tissue Paper

Shown below and on page 72.

- Stamp cowboy hats and stars onto the background of this tissue paper as shown.

▲ Western Tissue Paper
- Showing a closeup of the stamping detail.

73

Wrapping Papers

WRAPPING PAPERS

Shown on pages 74-81.

These wrapping papers can be made from any paper, but the ones shown were made from coated (glossy) paper and kraft paper.

To begin, cut the paper to the appropriate size for the gift to be wrapped.

Any background can be applied over the paper as desired.

Then, additional detailing can be stamped or embossed directly onto the paper or stamped or embossed onto sticker paper, cut out, and adhered to the paper.

Photo Frame Wrapping Paper

Shown on page 74.

- Stamp several wood frames and several snowflakes onto sticker paper and cut out.
- Place the wood frame stickers on a cutting mat. Carefully cut out the insides of the wood frames as shown with a sharp craft knife. These openings in the stickers dictate the position of the color-copied photos to be placed behind them.
- Crop the photos to fit the openings in the frames and adhere them in place on the back of the stickers.
- Place the wood frame stickers on the background of white coated paper. Stamp snowflakes between the frames, then place the snowflake stickers, overlapping the photos as shown.

Congratulations! Wrapping Paper

Shown at right and on page 74.

- Repeatedly stamp "Congratulations!", colorful balloons, and small stars onto the background of white coated paper.

Happy Birthday! Wrapping Paper

Shown above.

- Repeatedly stamp "Happy Birthday!" onto the background of white coated paper.

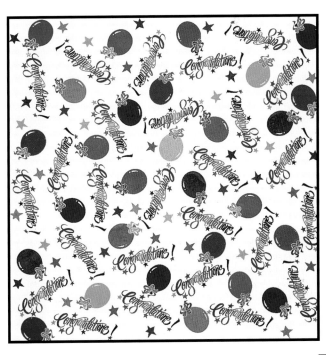

Floral
Wrapping Paper
Shown above.

- Repeatedly stamp various flowers onto the background of white coated paper.

Floral Frame
Wrapping Paper
Shown above.

- Repeatedly stamp frames onto the background of white coated paper. Stamp a flower pot, at one end of each frame, directly onto the paper.
- Stamp flowers onto sticker paper, cut out, and adhere to the paper. Make certain to place the flowers inside the flower pots.

Sunflower
Wrapping Paper
Shown at left.

- Draw dotted lines in a checkerboard pattern onto the background of blue coated paper with a white ballpoint correction pen as shown.
- Stamp several sunflowers onto sticker paper, cut out, and adhere to the paper as shown.

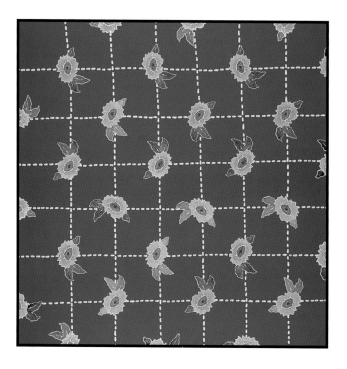

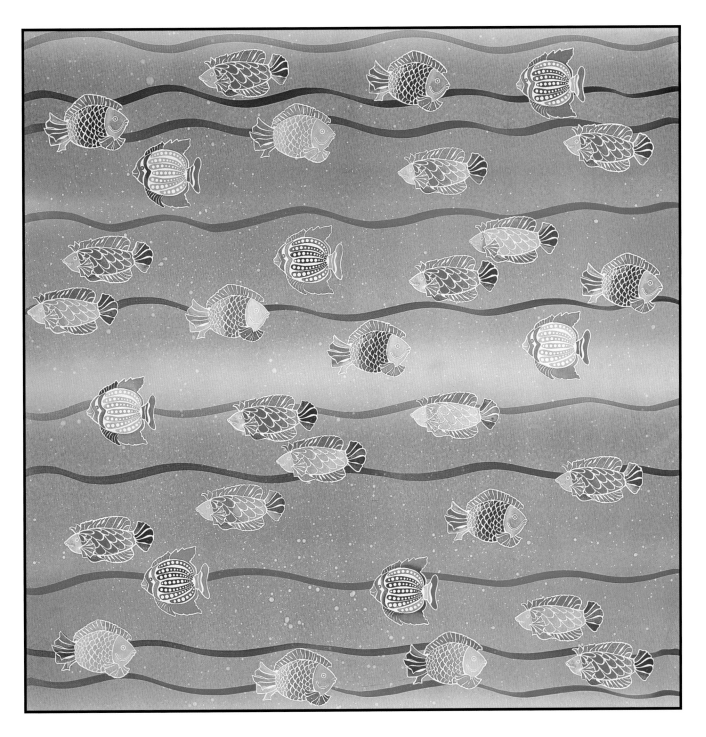

Rainbow Fish Wrapping Paper

Shown above.

- Brayer a rainbow effect onto the background of white coated paper with a rainbow pad and black foam brayer.

- Spray with a light mist of water and allow to dry thoroughly.

- Draw wavy lines horizontally across the brayered background at various intervals with colored pigment markers.

- Stamp assorted tropical fish onto sticker paper, cut out, and adhere to the paper as shown.

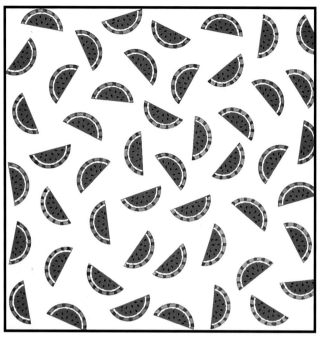

Watermelon Wrapping Paper

Shown above.

- Repeatedly stamp watermelon slices onto the background of white coated paper.

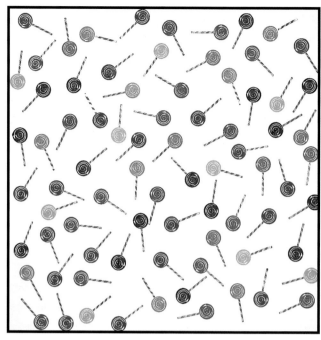

Lollypop Wrapping Paper

Shown above.

- Repeatedly stamp lollypops onto the background of white coated paper.

Crayon Heart Wrapping Paper

Shown at left and on page 74.

- Repeatedly stamp colorful hearts and crayons onto the background of white coated paper.
- Write the "color names" of each crayon inside each crayon label with colored pigment markers.

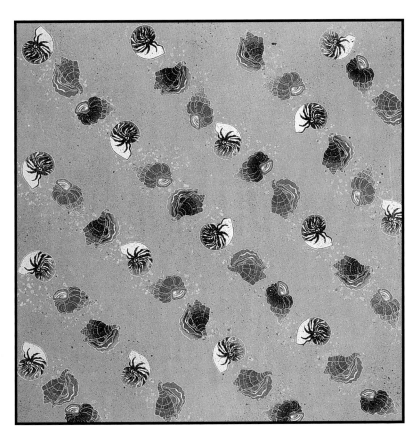

Seashell Wrapping Paper
Shown at left.

- Spatter black and white ink onto the background of recycled paper with a twisting spatter brush.
- Stamp rows of splatters with a white pigment ink pad.
- Stamp several seashells onto sticker paper, cut out, and adhere to the paper in diagonal rows.

Snowflake Wrapping Paper
Shown at right.

- Repeatedly emboss snowflakes onto the background of black uncoated paper with silver ink and embossing powder as shown.

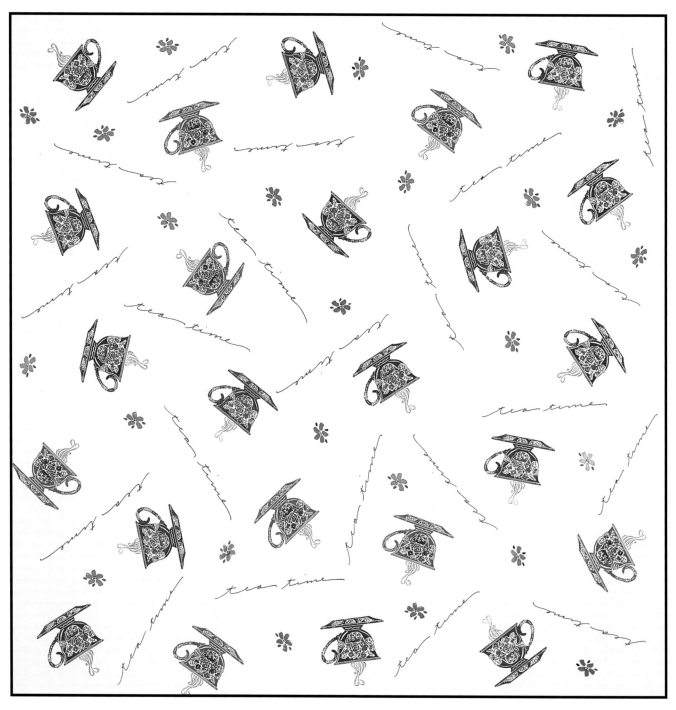

Tea Time
Wrapping Paper
Shown above.

- Repeatedly stamp tea cups and small flowers onto the background of white coated paper.
- Write "tea time" in various directions as shown with a colored pigment marker.

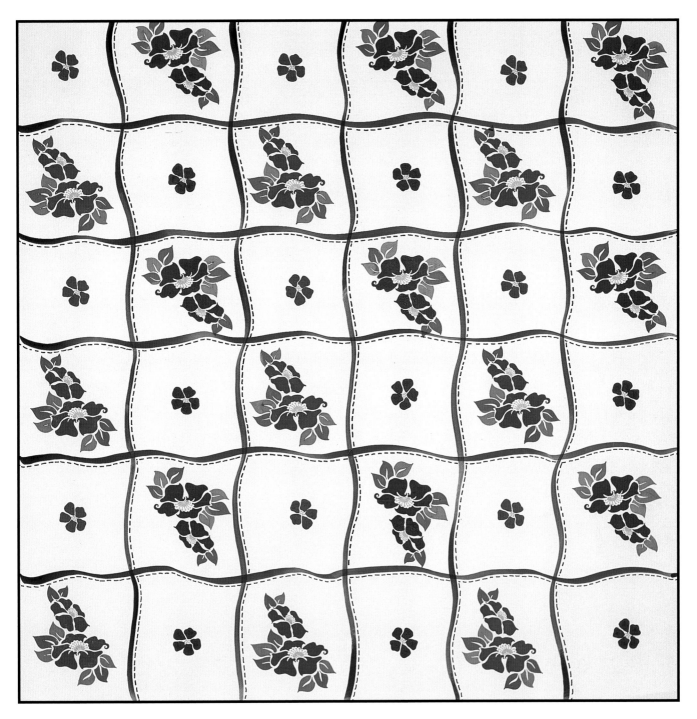

Floral Square Wrapping Paper

Shown above.

- Draw wavy lines horizontally and vertically across the background of white coated paper with dual-tip blue and purple pigment markers to create squares. Pull the markers across the paper, twisting with varying pressure as the lines are drawn, with the brush tip of each marker.

- Draw tiny coordinating stitch-lines on one side of the lines with the small tips of the same markers.

- Stamp large flower clusters and small flowers alternately inside each square as shown.

Placemat and Napkin

PLACEMATS
Shown on page 82.

These placemats can be made in any size, but the one shown measures 11" high x 17" wide. This is considered an ideal size because cardstock can be purchased precut to that size.

Placemats are always used horizontally and the placemat shown has been made from coated (glossy) cardstock, which gives a nice finished look.

The cardstock should be placed on a flat, padded surface. To begin, the size of the placemat must be determined. Once the cardstock has been cut, any background can be applied over the cardstock on one or both sides as desired. Applying a background on both sides allows the placemat to be reversible.

Then, additional detailing can be stamped directly onto the cardstock or stamped onto sticker paper, cut out, and adhered to the cardstock. For this application, embossing is not recommended.

When several identical placemats are desired, it is easiest to work in an assembly-line fashion.

Daisy Placemat
Shown on page 82.

- Draw lines in opposite diagonal directions onto the background of white coated cardstock with dual-tip colored pigment markers. Pull the markers across the cardstock, twisting with varying pressure as the lines are drawn, with the brush tip of each marker.
- Draw tiny coordinating stitch-lines on both sides of the lines with the small tips of the same markers.
- Stamp flowers in rows directly onto the cardstock as shown.
- If desired, stamp flowers onto sticker paper, cut out, and adhere to the cardstock, arranging as desired.
- If the placemats are to be used repeatedly, they need to be laminated and trimmed. This will allow the surface of the placemat to be wiped clean after each use.

NAPKINS
Shown on page 82.

The napkins chosen for stamping purposes can be any size (beverage, luncheon, or dinner), but they should be a good quality paper with a smooth surface.

The napkin should be opened up to a single thickness and placed on a flat surface. To begin, scrap paper should be placed underneath the napkin to absorb the ink that will bleed through.

Stamping and detailing can be done on one of the "outside" panels of the open napkin. For this application, embossing is not recommended and the use of sticker paper would make the napkin too heavy.

Once the ink has thoroughly dried, the napkin can be refolded. If the napkin is refolded before the ink has dried, the ink will bleed through to the other panels of the napkin.

When several identical napkins are desired, it is easiest to work in an assembly-line fashion.

Daisy Napkin
Shown on page 82.

- Open up a white dinner-sized napkin and stamp flowers directly onto one of the "outside" panels of the napkin.
- Stamp "dots" around the flowers as shown with the eraser-end of a new pencil.
- If desired, personalize each napkin with colored pigment markers.
- When the ink is thoroughly dry, refold the napkin.

Potted Placecards, Floral Toothpicks, and Potpourri Envelopes

POTTED PLACECARDS

Shown on page 84.

These potted placecards are embellished and personalized placecards that have been cut to fit inside tiny clay flower pots.

To begin, choose tiny clay flower pots and cut a piece of coated (glossy) cardstock that is at least twice as wide and about two and one-half times as tall as the flower pots. One flower pot and one piece of cut cardstock are needed for each potted placecard.

The flowers can be stamped or embossed directly onto the cardstock near the top edges. If desired, additional flowers can be stamped or embossed onto sticker paper and cut out. The flower stickers are then arranged over the flowers that have been stamped or embossed directly onto the cardstock.

Next, a banner for each placecard can be stamped or embossed onto sticker paper and cut out. Using colored pigment calligraphy markers, one guest's name can be written inside each banner to personalize each placecard.

The banner stickers are placed over the stems of the flowers.

The cardstock is then cut away around the flowers and sides of the banners, but the bottom of the cardstock is left untouched.

Now, the bottom of the cardstock can be carefully cut away at an angle to match the angle of the flower pots. The angled sides are trimmed, a little at a time, until the cardstock neatly fits inside the flower pots.

The bottom of the banners help balance and secure the placecards in place.

Add dried moss or crinkled paper "grass" to fill each flower pot.

Potted placecards can be made using the same flower for each one or different flowers for each one, depending on the mood and the occasion.

When several potted placecards are desired, it is easiest to work in an assembly-line fashion.

Spring Flower Potted Placecards

Shown on page 84.

- Cut white coated cardstock to an appropriate size for the clay flower pots being used.

- Stamp various flowers directly onto the cardstock, then stamp additional flowers onto sticker paper, cut out, and adhere to the cardstock on top of the stamped flowers.

- Stamp banners onto sticker paper, cut out, and personalize with colored pigment calligraphy markers.

- Place the banners over the stems of the flowers.

- The excess cardstock around the flowers and banners should be cut away and the bottoms trimmed to fit inside the flower pots.

- Add dried moss or crinkled paper "grass" to fill each flower pot.

FLORAL TOOTHPICKS

Shown on page 84.

These floral toothpicks are embellished toothpicks that can be used as hors'doeuvre picks for any special occasion.

To begin, one flower can be stamped or embossed onto sticker paper and cut out for each toothpick needed.

The bottom of each flower sticker is then peeled open enough to place a toothpick inside between the front and the removable backing. Once the toothpick has been secured, burnish the fronts and backs of the sticker paper together.

Floral toothpicks can be made using the same flower for each one or different flowers for each one, depending on the mood and the occasion.

Zinnia Toothpicks

Shown on page 84.

- Stamp zinnias in various colors onto sticker paper and cut out.
- Peel open the bottom of each flower sticker and place a toothpick inside. Once secure, burnish the fronts and backs of each sticker together.

POTPOURRI ENVELOPES

Shown on page 84.

These potpourri envelopes can be made in any size, but the one shown measures $4^3/_4$" high x $3^1/_2$" wide. It has been made from coated (glossy) cardstock because it folds well and can withstand the weight of the stamped embellishments.

To begin, the size of the potpourri envelope must be determined. Use the Potpourri Envelope Pattern on page 87. Once the cardstock has been cut, in this instance 6" x $7^1/_4$", a seed packet can be stamped or embossed directly onto the cardstock, centered, about $^5/_8$" away from the long edge of the cardstock.

Using a colored pigment calligraphy marker, "Potpourri" is handwritten inside the upper banner on the seed packet.

Then, the cardstock is scored just outside all four stamped edges to allow the cardstock to be neatly folded.

The envelope is then opened up and placed on a cutting mat. A sharp craft knife should be used to carefully cut out the center of the seed packet.

If desired, do not remove the center of the seed packet. Instead, a series of flowers can be stamped or embossed onto sticker paper and cut out. These flowers can then be arranged in the center of the seed packet. Make certain to overlap the edges of each flower in at least two or three places for stability. When arranged as desired, the areas around and between the flowers should be cut out with a sharp craft knife.

Next, a piece of netting is adhered behind the cut-out window in the envelope with an appropriate adhesive.

The envelope is folded, using the scored lines, as shown in the pattern. Once folded, the long side flaps are adhered together, then the bottom flap is adhered in place.

The envelope is filled with potpourri and the top flap adhered in place.

When several potpourri envelopes are desired, it is easiest to work in an assembly-line fashion.

Zinnia Potpourri Envelope

Shown on page 84.

- Cut white coated cardstock according to the Potpourri Envelope Pattern below.
- Stamp a seed packet and zinnias directly onto the cardstock.

- Write the word "Potpourri" inside the upper banner on the seed packet as shown with a pink pigment calligraphy marker.
- Score the edges around the seed packet to allow the cardstock to be neatly folded.
- Open up the envelope and place it on a cutting mat. Carefully cut out the center of the seed packet, around the zinnias, as shown with a sharp craft knife.

- Adhere a piece of netting behind the cut-out window in the envelope with an appropriate adhesive.
- Fold the envelope, using the scored lines, as shown in the pattern. Once folded, adhere the long side flaps together with an appropriate adhesive, then adhere the bottom flap in place.
- Fill the envelope with potpourri and adhere the top flap in place.

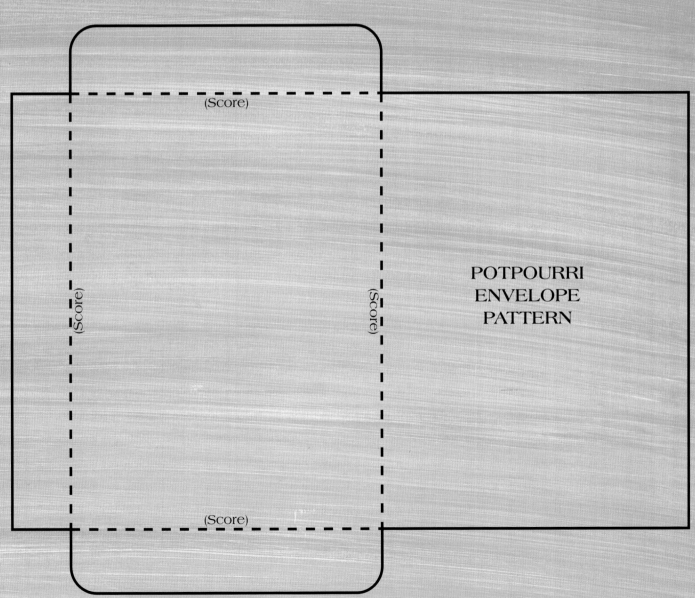

(Score)

(Score)

(Score)

(Score)

POTPOURRI
ENVELOPE
PATTERN

Journal and Paper Pad

JOURNALS
Shown on page 88.

Journals can be purchased in many sizes, but the one shown measures 8" high x 5½" wide.

To begin, choose a journal that will best serve your needs. Make certain the cover of the journal can be stamped.

Once the journal has been chosen, any background can be applied over the cover.

Then, additional detailing can be stamped or embossed directly onto the cover or stamped or embossed onto sticker paper, cut out, and adhered to the cover.

Stickers can also be used to add color and dimension. When adding stickers — preprinted or made from sticker paper — overlap as desired to add interest.

My Journal
Shown on page 88.

- Brayer a rainbow effect onto the background of the white coated cardstock that is positioned behind a clear cover with a rainbow pad and black foam brayer. If this seems difficult, brayer the background onto sticker paper, cut out, and adhere to the cardstock as desired.
- Stamp three assorted tropical fish, two assorted seashells, seaweed, one hermit crab, one sea horse, and one banner onto sticker paper and cut out.
- Place the tropical fish, seashells, seaweed, hermit crab, and sea horse stickers over the brayered background as shown.
- Write the words "My Journal" inside the banner with a purple pigment calligraphy marker.
- Place the banner sticker on the outside of the clear cover.
- Add bubbles on the brayered background as shown with a white opaque pen.

Dee's Paper Pad
Shown on page 88.

- Stamp a single flower directly onto each sheet of white 20 lb. bond paper as shown.
- In this instance, the name was printed on each sheet at the time the pad was custom made.

PAPER PADS
Shown on page 88.

These paper pads can be made in any size, but the one shown measures 6" high x 4" wide. Paper pads can be purchased in a variety of sizes or can be custom made at any printing shop. The paper pad shown has been made from 20 lb. bond paper, which is ideal for note writing and is available in a variety of colors.

To begin, the size of the paper pad must be determined. Once the paper pad(s) has been purchased or custom made, any image can be stamped directly onto each sheet. For this application, embossing is not recommended.

The stamped images can be placed any place on the notepad — in one corner, along the top, along the bottom — the possibilities are endless! For variety, a different image can be stamped on each sheet.

If personalization is desired, the name can be handwritten, stamped, or printed on the sheets at the time the pad is custom made.

Window Bags

WINDOW BAGS

Shown on page 90.

These window bags can be made in any size, but the ones shown measure 6" high x 5½" wide. The window bags shown have been made from coated (glossy) cardstock.

To begin, the size of the window bag must be determined. Once the cardstock has been cut, in this instance 5½" x 17", any background can be applied over the cardstock.

Then, the cardstock is scored at six inches, nine inches, and fifteen inches to allow the cardstock to be neatly folded.

The window will be in the first 6" section. A large open image can be stamped or embossed directly onto the cardstock or stamped or embossed onto sticker paper, cut out, and adhered to the cardstock. Once the inside of the open image has been cut out and removed, the window will reveal the contents of the bag on the inside of the folded cardstock.

Then, additional detailing on the front can be stamped or embossed directly onto the cardstock or stamped or embossed onto sticker paper, cut out, and adhered to the cardstock.

Stickers can also be used to add color and dimension. When adding stickers — preprinted or made from sticker paper — overlap as desired to add interest.

The cardstock is folded, using the scored lines. Trim the end nearest the 2" top flap as desired with decorative-edged scissors. Once folded, the trimmed top flap can be adhered in place with an appropriate adhesive or stapled.

Next, fill a 5"-wide cellophane bag with treats or potpourri and fold the top over to close. The cellophane bag is placed inside the cardstock "case" and adhered in place with an appropriate adhesive.

When several window bags are desired, it is easiest to work in an assembly-line fashion.

Potpourri Window Bag

Shown on page 90.

- Cut white coated cardstock 5½" wide x 17" high for a folded "case" of 5½" wide x 6" high.

- Brayer a rainbow effect onto the background of white coated cardstock with a rainbow pad and black foam brayer. Lightly mist the brayer with water to create the watercolor effect.

- Stamp a seed packet onto sticker paper, cut out, and adhere to the first 6" section. Make certain to leave enough space for the 2" top flap to be folded over.

- Write the word "Potpourri" inside the upper banner on the seed packet as shown with a pink pigment calligraphy marker.

- Score the cardstock at six inches, nine inches, and fifteen inches to allow the cardstock to be neatly folded.

- Open up the cardstock and place it on a cutting mat. Carefully cut out the center of the seed packet as shown with a sharp craft knife.

- Fold the cardstock, using the scored lines. Once folded, trim the 2" top flap as desired with decorative-edged scissors and adhere in place with an appropriate adhesive.

- Fill a 5"-wide cellophane bag with potpourri and fold the top over to close.

- Place the filled bag inside the cardstock "case" and adhere in place.

Candied Pretzel Window Bag

Shown on page 90.

- Cut white coated cardstock 5½" wide x 17" high for a folded "case" of 5½" wide x 6" high.
- Brayer a rainbow effect onto the background with a rainbow pad and black foam brayer.

- Stamp a candy jar onto sticker paper, cut out, and adhere to the first 6" section. Make certain to leave enough space for the 2" top flap to be folded over.
- Score the cardstock at six inches, nine inches, and fifteen inches to allow the cardstock to be neatly folded.
- Open up the cardstock and place it on a cutting mat. Carefully cut out the center of the candy jar as shown with a sharp craft knife.

- Fold the cardstock, using the scored lines. Once folded, trim the 2" top flap as desired with decorative-edged scissors and adhere in place with an appropriate adhesive.
- Fill a 5"-wide cellophane bag with candied pretzels and fold the top over to close.
- Place the filled bag inside the cardstock "case" and adhere in place.

Chocolate Chip Cookie Window Bag

Shown on page 90.

- Cut white coated cardstock 5½" wide x 17" high for a folded "case" of 5½" wide x 6" high.
- Brayer a rainbow effect onto the background with a rainbow pad and black foam brayer.
- Stamp a basket onto sticker paper, cut out, and adhere to the first 6" section. Make certain to leave enough space for the 2" top flap to be folded over.

- Stamp one ribbon tag onto sticker paper and cut out.
- Stamp the words "To:" and "From:" inside the ribbon tag as shown.
- Score the cardstock at six inches, nine inches, and fifteen inches to allow the cardstock to be neatly folded.
- Open up the cardstock and place it on a cutting mat. Carefully cut out the top of the basket, inside the handle as shown, with a sharp craft knife. Small areas in the body of the basket can also be removed.
- Cut one small slit on each side of the basket handle and thread a piece of rib-

bon through the slits. Tie the ribbon into a small bow and trim each ribbon end at an angle.
- Fold the cardstock, using the scored lines. Once folded, trim the 2" top flap as desired with decorative-edged scissors and adhere in place with an appropriate adhesive.
- Place the ribbon tag sticker, overlapping the top flap as shown.
- Fill a 5"-wide cellophane bag with small chocolate chip cookies and fold the top over to close.
- Place the filled bag inside the cardstock "case" and adhere in place.

Stationery Portfolio

STATIONERY PORTFOLIO
Shown on page 93.

These stationery portfolios can be made in any size, but the one shown measures $9\frac{1}{4}$" high x $6\frac{1}{2}$" wide. It was made from cardstock measuring 11" high x 17" wide. This is considered an ideal size because cardstock can be purchased precut to that size.

The stationery portfolio shown has been made from coated (glossy) cardstock, which gives a nice finished look.

To begin, the size of the portfolio must be determined. Once the cardstock has been cut, any background can be applied over the cardstock on one or both sides as desired.

Then, additional detailing can be stamped directly onto the cardstock or stamped onto sticker paper, cut out, and adhered to the cardstock.

The cardstock is scored along one long edge $1\frac{3}{4}$" from the bottom, $\frac{3}{4}$" from both short edges, $6\frac{1}{2}$" and 13" from the first scored line on the left to allow the cardstock to be neatly folded.

Trim the two top corners as shown in the Stationery Portfolio Diagram below. The portfolio is folded, using the scored lines. Fold both short edges in, then fold the bottom up, and secure at each end with an appropriate adhesive. Fold along the remaining scored lines to create one small pocket in the flap of the portfolio and two larger pockets on the inside.

Next, decorate stationery, envelopes, and stickers with stamped images to match the outside of the portfolio. Place the stationery and the envelopes inside the large pockets on the inside of the portfolio and add stamped stickers and/or postage stamps inside the small pocket. To close, fold the small flap over and add a button and loop or other closure with an appropriate adhesive.

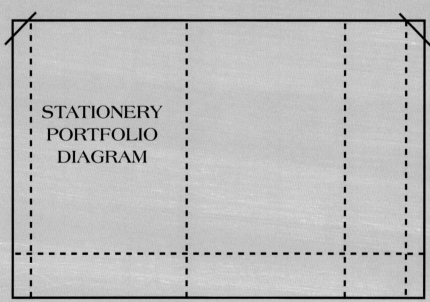

STATIONERY
PORTFOLIO
DIAGRAM

Floral Stationery Portfolio

Shown on page 93 and below.

- Brayer flowers onto the background of white coated cardstock with a soft rubber brayer, then stamp additional flowers on top of the brayered ones.
- Spatter several colors of ink onto the background with a twisting spatter brush.
- Stamp several flowers onto sticker paper, cut out, and adhere to the cardstock.
- Score the cardstock along one long edge 1³/₄" from the bottom, ³/₄" from both short edges, 6¹/₂" and 13" from the first scored line on the left to allow the cardstock to be neatly folded.
- Trim the two top corners as shown in the Stationery Portfolio Diagram on page 94.
- Fold the cardstock, using the scored lines. Once folded, secure each end with an appropriate adhesive.
- Decorate stationery, envelopes, and stickers to match the outside of the portfolio.
- Place the stationery, envelopes, and stickers inside the pockets on the inside of the portfolio.
- To close, fold the small flap over and add a button and loop closure with an appropriate adhesive.

Floral Stationery

Shown on page 93.

- Cut white coated paper 6¹/₄" wide x 9" high. One sheet is needed for each sheet of stationery desired.
- Stamp flowers onto the background, in opposite corners, as shown.
- Draw one wide, wiggly line around each sheet, ¹/₄" from all outside edges, with a green pigment marker. Draw a thin, wiggly line, just inside the wide line, with a blue pigment marker. Draw a small dot border, just inside the thin line, with a red pigment marker.
- When stamping sheets of stationery, it is easiest to work in an assembly-line fashion.

▲ Button and Loop Closure
- Showing a closeup of the button and loop closure.

Floral Envelopes

Shown on page 93.

- Stamp flowers onto the front of a white coated A6 envelope, in opposite corners, as shown.
- Draw one very thin, wiggly line around each envelope, 1" from all outside edges with a green pigment marker to create a label in the middle of the envelope. Draw a wide, wiggly line, just inside the very thin line, with a blue pigment marker. Draw another line, just inside the wide line, with a red pigment marker.
- When stamping envelopes, it is easiest to work in an assembly-line fashion.

Floral Stickers

Shown on page 93.

- Cut sticker paper into 2¹/₄" x 8¹/₄" strips to fit inside the small pocket on the inside of the portfolio.
- Stamp flowers directly onto sticker paper.
- When ready to use, cut out and adhere as desired.

Recipe Box and Tabbed Dividers

RECIPE BOXES

Shown on page 96.

Recipe boxes can be purchased in many sizes, but the one shown measures $5\frac{1}{4}$" wide x 4" high x $3\frac{1}{2}$" deep. They also can be purchased premade from many different mediums: plastic, wood, heavy cardboard.

To begin, choose a recipe box that will best serve your needs.

Once the recipe box has been chosen, and depending on the medium from which the box is made, special stamping inks may be needed to insure the stamped images will adhere to the surface of the box. In addition, special ink solvents may be needed for cleaning up mistakes, smears, and general cleanup of rubber stamps.

These special stamping inks generally dry quickly, but make certain to be extremely careful not to smear the ink as you continue stamping.

Simple images can be stamped directly onto the recipe box. If desired, images can be stamped onto sticker paper, cut out, and adhered to the recipe box.

Garden Fresh Recipe Box

Shown on page 96.

- Squeeze a small puddle of each color of stamping ink formulated to be used on plastic onto a disposable palette. If desired, ink colors can be mixed at this time.
- Apply the stamping ink onto the rubber stamp with a wedge sponge. Use a different wedge sponge for each color.
- If necessary, lightly blot off excess stamping ink onto a paper towel.
- Practice a few times before actually beginning to stamp on the recipe box because the rubber stamp may move on the slick surface.
- Stamp carrots directly onto the recipe box, overlapping as shown. Be careful not to smear the stamping ink as you continue stamping.
- Immediately cleanup all rubber stamps with the special ink solvent while the stamping ink dries.

TABBED DIVIDERS

Shown on pages 96, 98 & 99.

Recipe boxes generally come with tabbed dividers that fit inside. The ones shown have been made from coated (glossy) cardstock.

To begin, determine how many dividers are needed. Once the dividers have been cut, any background can be applied over the dividers on one or both sides as desired.

An image is then stamped directly onto the divider or stamped onto sticker paper, cut out, and adhered to the divider.

Stickers can also be used to add color and dimension. When adding stickers — preprinted or made from sticker paper — overlap as desired to add interest.

Using different stamped images for each divider makes them colorful and fun. Make certain to coordinate the stamped images with the food categories being described on each tabbed divider.

The names of the food categories can be handwritten directly onto the tabs of the dividers with pigment markers.

Embellished Tabbed Dividers

Shown on
pages 96, 98 & 99.

- Shown smaller than actual size.

- Brayer a rainbow effect onto the background of white coated cardstock tabbed dividers with a rainbow pad and black foam brayer. Use a different color scheme for each divider to add interest.

- Stamp food images that coordinate with each food category onto sticker paper and cut out.

- Place the food image stickers on the tabbed dividers as shown.

- Write the names of the food categories on each tab with a black pigment marker.

Fruits

Veggies

Seafood

Drinks

Soups

Desserts

Recipe and Special Occasion Packets and Hanging Heart Box

RECIPE AND SPECIAL OCCASION PACKETS

Shown on page 100.

These packets can be made in any size, but the ones shown were made from 5"-wide cellophane bags with toppers made from cardstock measuring 5" wide x 7" high for a folded topper size of 5" wide x 3¹/₂" high.

To begin, the size of the packets must be determined. Once the cardstock for the topper has been cut, any background can be applied over the cardstock.

The cardstock is scored in half width-wise to allow the cardstock to be neatly folded.

Then, additional detailing can be stamped directly onto the cardstock or stamped onto sticker paper, cut out, and adhered to the cardstock.

Words, greetings, recipes, etc., can be stamped or handwritten on the front of the toppers with colored pigment markers as desired.

Next, fill a 5"-wide cellophane bag with desired contents and fold the top over to close. The cellophane bag is placed in between the cardstock topper and is stapled to the back of the topper only. The front of the topper is adhered in place with an appropriate adhesive.

When several packets are desired, it is easiest to work in an assembly-line fashion.

Chili Seasoning Packet

Shown on page 100.

- Cut cardstock 5" wide x 7" high for a folded topper size of 5" wide x 3¹/₂" high.

- No stamping or special techniques were used on this background.

- Stamp two chili peppers onto sticker paper and cut out.

- Score the cardstock in half width-wise to allow the cardstock to be neatly folded.

- Draw a wide, wiggly lined border around the front side of the topper with a brown pigment marker. Draw a very thin, wiggly line, just inside the wide line, with a red pigment marker. Draw a small dot border, just inside the very thin line, with a red pigment marker.

- Place the chili pepper stickers in opposite corners as shown.

- Write the recipe for "Chili Seasoning" inside the wiggly-lined border as shown with a green pigment marker.

- Fill a 5"-wide cellophane bag with chili seasoning made from the given recipe and fold the top over to close.

- Place the cellophane bag in between the cardstock topper and staple it to the back of the topper only. Adhere the front of the topper in place with an appropriate adhesive.

CHILI SEASONING

- 1 teaspoon cumin
- 1 teaspoon garlic
- 1 teaspoon red pepper
- 2 teaspoons seasoning salt
- 2 tablespoons chili powder
- 2 teaspoons onion powder
- 1 tablespoon sugar

Mix all dry ingredients together and place in a 5"-wide cellophane bag.

HANGING HEART BOX

Shown on page 100.

These hanging heart boxes can be made in any size, but the one shown measures 4" wide x 4½" high. It has been made from cardstock because it folds well and can withstand the weight of the stamped embellishments.

To begin, the size of the heart box must be determined. Use the Hanging Heart Box pattern on page 105. Once the cardstock has been cut, any background can be applied over the cardstock.

Then, additional detailing can be stamped or embossed directly onto the cardstock or stamped or embossed onto sticker paper, cut out, and adhered to the cardstock.

The cardstock is scored as shown in the pattern to allow the cardstock to be folded nicely. The heart box is folded, using the scored lines, and the side flap is adhered with an appropriate adhesive. Make certain the little flap is tucked underneath the side flap.

Next, holes are punched in the sides near the top to allow string or ribbon to be threaded. Bows or knots can be used on the inside or the outside of the heart box.

The heart box is filled with desired contents.

When several hanging heart boxes are desired, it is easiest to work in an assembly-line fashion.

Bridal Bird Seed Packet

Shown on page 100.

- Cut white coated cardstock 5" wide x 7" high for a folded topper size of 5" wide x 3½" high.
- Brayer a rainbow effect onto the front side of the topper with a rainbow pad and black foam brayer.
- Lightly mist brayered background with a spray bottle to create the "speckled" effect.
- Stamp two doves and one banner onto sticker paper and cut out.
- Write the names of the bride and groom inside the banner sticker with a pink pigment marker.
- Score the cardstock in half width-wise to allow the cardstock to be neatly folded.
- Place the dove stickers as shown, then place the banner sticker.
- Fill a 5"-wide cellophane bag with bird seed and fold the top over to close.
- Place the cellophane bag in between the cardstock topper and staple it to the back of the topper only. Adhere the front of the topper in place with an appropriate adhesive.

Rainbow Heart Box

Shown on page 100.

- Cut white coated cardstock according to the Hanging Heart Box Pattern on page 105.
- Brayer a rainbow effect onto the background with a rainbow pad and black foam brayer.
- Stamp a greeting directly onto the cardstock.
- Stamp one ribbon onto sticker paper and cut out.
- Score the heart box as shown in the pattern to allow the cardstock to be neatly folded.
- Fold the heart box, using the scored lines. Once folded, adhere the side flap, over the little flap, with an appropriate adhesive.
- Place the ribbon sticker as shown.
- Punch holes in the sides near the top and thread ribbon through. Tie knots at each end on the outside of the heart box.
- Fill the heart box with dried flowers.

102

Pillow Boxes

PILLOW BOX

Shown on page 103.

These pillow boxes can be made in any size, but the ones shown measure 4" wide x 6½" high. They have been made from coated (glossy) cardstock because it folds well and can withstand the weight of the stamped embellishments.

To begin, the size of the pillow box must be determined. Use the Pillow Box pattern on page 105. Once the cardstock has been cut, any background can be applied over the cardstock.

A frame is stamped onto sticker paper and cut out. It is adhered, centered, in the section next to the long narrow flap.

The cardstock is scored as shown in the Pillow Box Pattern to allow the cardstock to be neatly folded. The pillow box is folded, using the scored lines.

The pillow box is then opened up and placed on a cutting mat. A sharp craft knife should be used to carefully cut out the center of the frame.

Next, a piece of netting or acetate is then adhered behind the cut-out frame in the pillow box with an appropriate adhesive.

The pillow box is folded, using the scored lines, as shown in the pattern. Once folded, the long narrow flap is adhered over the back. The football-shaped sections on the bottom are pushed in by pinching on the scored lines to fold. If desired, secure in position with an appropriate adhesive.

The pillow box is filled with treats or potpourri and the football-shaped sections on the top are closed as the bottom ones were.

When several pillow boxes are desired, it is easiest to work in an assembly-line fashion.

Rose & Autumn Leaf Pillow Boxes

Shown on page 103.

- Cut white coated cardstock according to the Pillow Box pattern on page 105.
- Brayer roses or autumn leaves onto the front of the cardstock with a soft rubber brayer, then stamp additional roses or autumn leaves on top of the brayered ones.
- Stamp one decorative frame onto sticker paper, cut out, and adhere to the cardstock as shown.
- Score the cardstock to allow it to be neatly folded.
- Open up the pillow box and place it on a cutting mat. Carefully cut out the center of the frame as shown with a sharp craft knife.
- Adhere a piece of netting or acetate behind the cut-out frame in the pillow box with an appropriate adhesive.
- Fold the pillow box as shown in the Pillow Box Pattern on page 105, using the scored lines. Once folded, adhere the long narrow flap over the back. Fold by pushing the football-shaped sections on the bottom in by pinching on the scored lines. If desired, secure with an appropriate adhesive.
- Fill the pillow box with treats or potpourri and close the top football-shaped sections as the bottom ones were.
- If desired, tie ribbon or raffia around each pillow box.

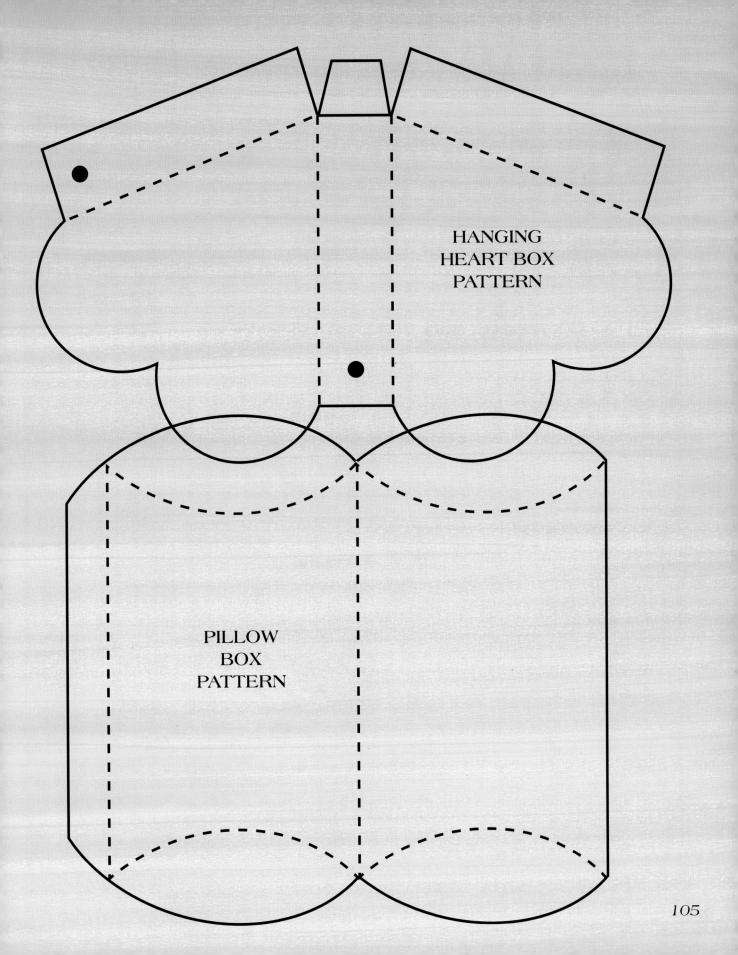

HANGING
HEART BOX
PATTERN

PILLOW
BOX
PATTERN

Photo Frame Necklace

PHOTO FRAME NECKLACE

Shown on page 106.

This photo frame necklace can be made in any length and with as many framed photos as desired.

To begin, the size and length of the chain and the number of photos to be used must be determined.

Because this is a photo frame necklace, a frame for each photo is stamped onto sticker paper and cut out. The same frame stamp can be used for each photo or for variety; try using several different frame stamps. Once the insides of the frames have been cut out and removed, each frame will accentuate the photo that is placed behind it.

After each photo is secured in position on the back of the photo frame sticker, color-copy each framed photo at a reduction of approximately 40%.

Then, cut out each image, leaving a $1/16$" white border around each photo frame.

Using a thick (10 ml) laminate, laminate each cut-out photo frame and cut out again, this time leaving a $1/16$" clear laminate border around each photo frame.

At the top of each small framed photo, a tiny hole must be punched to accommodate a metal jump ring. An awl or a heavy needle works well for this purpose.

Next, attach each framed photo to the chain with the metal jump rings. Using three jump rings on each photo frame will assist in getting the photos to dangle straight, but freely.

Grandma's Framed Photo Brag Necklace

Shown on page 106.

- Use a 24" chain (necklace) that will accommodate the size of the metal jump rings being used.
- Stamp various frames onto sticker paper and cut out. One frame is needed for each photo to be used.
- One at a time, place the frame stickers on a cutting mat. Carefully cut out the inside of each frame as shown with a sharp craft knife. This opening in each sticker dictates the position of the color-copied photo to be placed behind it.
- In this instance, the photos were color-copied in black-and-white mode so that all photos become "black and white."
- Crop each photo to fit the opening in the desired frame and adhere it in place on the back of the sticker. Choose frames that will coordinate with the photos to be used together. For example, a birthday cake frame with a photo of a birthday party, or a tent frame with a photo of a camping trip.
- Make a color-copy of each framed photo at a reduction of approximately 40%.
- Cut out each image, leaving a $1/16$" white border around each photo frame.
- Laminate each cut-out photo frame and cut out again, this time leaving a $1/16$" clear laminate border around each photo frame.
- Punch one tiny hole at the top of each small framed photo to accommodate the metal jump rings.
- Attach each framed photo to the chain with three metal jump rings.

Photo Frame Ornaments

PHOTO FRAME ORNAMENTS

Shown on page 108.

These photo frame ornaments can be made in any size, from any frame stamp, but all those shown were made from decorative frame stamps and are used vertically. They have been made from cardstock because it gives stability for hanging.

To begin, the size and design of the ornament must be determined.

Next, the color of the cardstock to be used for the background of the ornament must be determined.

Because these are photo frame ornaments, frames are then stamped or embossed directly onto the cardstock. A second piece of cardstock should be placed behind the stamped or embossed frames and temporarily secured into position. The frames are then cut out, along with the backing pieces, so

they are the exact shape. Once the inside of the stamped or embossed frames have been cut out and removed, the frames will accentuate the photos that are placed between the two pieces of cardstock. Do not cut out the inside of the frames to be used as the backing.

A piece of ribbon for hanging and a small ribbon bow were added at the top of each photo frame ornament for a festive look.

Victorian Photo Frame Ornaments

Shown on page 108.

- For each ornament, emboss a decorative frame onto black cardstock with gold or silver embossing inks and metallic powders.
- Place a second piece of black cardstock behind the embossed frames and temporarily secure them together.
- Cut out the frames at the same time so they are the exact shape. The frame in the back will be used as the backing of the ornament.
- One at a time, place the embossed frames on a cutting mat. Carefully cut out the inside of each frame as shown with a sharp craft knife. This opening in each frame dictates the position of the color-copied photo to be placed behind it.
- Crop the photos to fit the openings in the frames and adhere them in place on the back with an appropriate adhesive.
- Place the piece of cardstock backing on the back of the ornament and secure it in place with an appropriate adhesive.
- Add a piece of ribbon and a small ribbon bow at the top of each photo frame ornament for hanging.

Photo Frame Aprons and Mugs

PHOTO FRAME APRONS

Shown on page 110.

These photo frame aprons were made from purchased aprons that have been embellished with photo transfers. Make certain the apron fabric has some cotton content.

To begin, choose an apron that will best serve your needs.

Because these are photo frame aprons, the photos were cropped to fit inside stamped frames and were then color-copied, enlarged, and reversed onto fabric transfer film. The transfer film was then heat-pressed onto the fabric at a local T-shirt shop. It is best to call ahead to make certain the shop has the appropriate equipment to handle your request.

Transfer films are also available at some office supply stores that are compatible with computer ink jet printers.

Thanks, Teacher Apron

Shown on page 110.

- To create the artwork to be used on this apron, stamp one rope frame, one banner, and two apples onto sticker paper and cut out.
- Place the rope frame sticker on a cutting mat. Carefully cut out the inside of the rope frame as shown with a sharp craft knife. This opening in the sticker dictates the position of the color-copied photo to be placed behind it.
- Crop the photo to fit the opening in the frame and adhere it in place on the back of the sticker.
- Place the rope frame sticker as shown onto white cardstock, then place the banner and apple stickers.
- Write the words "Thanks, Teacher" inside the banner with a red pigment marker.
- Color-copy and reverse the artwork onto fabric transfer film. Make certain to enlarge or reduce the artwork to the desired size at this time.
- Heat-press the artwork onto a piece of cotton fabric.
- In this instance, the cotton fabric with the transferred artwork was quilted with cotton batting and then sewn onto the apron as shown.

Grandma's Pride & Joy Apron

Shown on page 110.

- To create the artwork to be used on this apron, stamp one wood frame, one bow, and one scroll onto sticker paper and cut out.
- Place the wood frame sticker on a cutting màt. Carefully cut out the inside of the wood frame as shown with a sharp craft knife. This opening in the sticker dictates the position of the color-copied photo to be placed behind it.
- Crop the photo to fit the opening in the frame and adhere it in place on the back of the sticker.
- Place the wood frame sticker as shown onto white cardstock, then place the bow and scroll stickers.
- Write the words "Grandma's Pride & Joy!" inside the scroll with a brown pigment calligraphy marker.
- Color-copy and reverse the artwork onto fabric transfer film. Make certain to enlarge or reduce the artwork to the desired size at this time.
- Heat-press the artwork onto a piece of cotton fabric.
- In this instance, the cotton fabric with the transferred artwork was made into a pocket and sewn onto the apron as shown.

PHOTO FRAME MUGS

Shown on page 110.

These photo frame mugs were made from purchased plastic insert mugs that have been embellished with framed photos.

To begin, use the insert that comes with the mug as a pattern and cut an insert from coated (glossy) card-stock. Once the cardstock has been cut, any background can be applied over the cardstock.

Because these are photo frame mugs, frames are then stamped directly onto the card-stock or stamped onto sticker paper, cut out, and adhered to the card-stock. Once the insides of the frames have been cut out and removed, the frames will accentuate the photos that are placed behind them.

Then, additional detailing can be stamped directly onto the card-stock or stamped onto sticker paper, cut out, and adhered to the card-stock. For this application, embossing is not recommended.

Stickers can also be used to add color and dimension. When adding stickers — preprinted or made from sticker paper — overlap as desired to add interest.

If desired, personalize each mug by stamping or handwriting names and/or words inside one or more stamped frames.

To assemble, follow the instructions that come with the mug.

Vacationing With Grandma Mug

Shown on page 110.

- Cut white coated cardstock, using the insert that comes with the mug as a pattern.
- Sponge wavy stripes onto the background with re-inkers and a compressed sponge.
- To create the artwork to be used inside this mug, stamp three wood frames onto sticker paper and cut out.
- Place the wood frame stickers on a cutting mat. Carefully cut out the insides of the wood frames as shown with a sharp craft knife. These openings in the stickers dictate the position of the color-copied photos to be placed behind them.
- Crop the photos to fit the openings in the frames and adhere them in place on the back of the stickers.
- Place the wood frame stickers onto the compressed sponge background as shown.
- Assemble the mug, following the instructions that come with the mug.

Cow-Boy Mug

Shown on page 110.

- Cut white coated cardstock, using the insert that comes with the mug as a pattern.
- Draw double-diagonal stripes onto the background with colored pigment markers.
- To create the artwork to be used inside this mug, stamp three cow frames onto sticker paper and cut out.
- Place the cow frame stickers on a cutting mat. Carefully cut out the insides of two of the cow frames as shown with a sharp craft knife. These openings in the stickers dictate the position of the color-copied photos to be placed behind them.
- Crop the photos to fit the openings in the frames and adhere them in place on the back of the stickers. Remove the outside border on one of the cow frames and stamp or write a greeting on the inside.
- Place the cow frame stickers onto the striped background as shown.
- Assemble the mug, following the instructions that come with the mug.

Photo Frame Mouse Pads

PHOTO FRAME MOUSE PADS

Shown on pages 113 & 115.

These photo frame mouse pads were made from purchased mouse pads that allow customizing. The two shown have been embellished with framed photos.

To begin, use the insert that comes with the mouse pad as a pattern and cut an insert from coated (glossy) cardstock. Once the cardstock has been cut, any background can be applied over the cardstock.

Because these are photo frame mouse pads, frames are then stamped directly onto the cardstock or stamped onto sticker paper, cut out, and adhered to the cardstock. Once the insides of the frames have been cut out and removed, the frames will accentuate the photos that are placed behind them.

Then, additional detailing can be stamped directly onto the cardstock or stamped onto sticker paper, cut out, and adhered to the cardstock. For this application, embossing cannot be done.

Stickers can also be used to add color and dimension. When adding stickers — preprinted or made from sticker paper — overlap as desired to add interest.

To assemble, follow the instructions that come with the mouse pad.

Tropical Fish Mouse Pad

Shown on page 113.

- Cut white coated cardstock, using the insert that comes with the mouse pad as a pattern.
- Brayer a watercolor effect over the background with markers and a sponge brayer.
- Brayer sea grass and field flowers onto the watercolor background with a soft rubber brayer, then stamp additional sea grass and field flowers on top of the brayered ones.
- Stamp one flyfishing "fly" directly onto the cardstock as shown.
- Stamp one porthole frame, seven assorted tropical fish, and nine assorted seashells onto sticker paper and cut out.
- Place the porthole frame sticker on a cutting mat. Carefully cut out the inside of the porthole frame as shown with a sharp craft knife. This opening in the sticker dictates the position of the color-copied photo to be placed behind it.
- Crop the photo to fit the opening in the frame and adhere it in place on the back of the sticker.
- Place the tropical fish and seashell stickers onto the cardstock as shown, then place the porthole frame sticker. Trim the tropical fish and seashells as necessary at the edges of the cardstock.
- Assemble the mouse pad, following the instructions that come with the mouse pad.

Military Mouse Pad

Shown above.

- Cut white coated cardstock, using the insert that comes with the mouse pad as a pattern.
- Brayer stripes in opposite diagonal directions onto the background of white coated cardstock with a soft rubber brayer to create a plaid background.

- Stamp three decorative frames onto sticker paper and cut out.
- Place the decorative frame stickers on a cutting mat. Carefully cut out the insides of the decorative frames as shown with a sharp craft knife. These openings in the stickers dictate the position of the color-copied photos to be placed behind them.

- Crop the photos to fit the openings in the frames and adhere them in place on the back of the stickers.
- Place the decorative frame stickers onto the cardstock as shown.
- Assemble the mouse pad, following the instructions that come with the mouse pad.

Photo Frame Bookmarks

PHOTO FRAME BOOKMARKS

Shown on pages 116-121.

These photo frame bookmarks can be made in any size and shape. They have been made from cardstock because it can withstand the weight of the stamped embellishments.

To begin, the size and shape of the bookmark must be determined.

Because these are photo frame bookmarks, a frame is stamped onto sticker paper and cut out. Then, an identical frame is stamped directly onto the cardstock without re-inking the stamp. Once the inside of the frame has been cut out and removed, the frame will accentuate the photo that is placed behind it.

Then, additional detailing on the front can be stamped or drawn directly onto the cardstock or stamped onto sticker paper, cut out, and adhered to the cardstock. For this application, embossing is not recommended.

In some instances, detailing may be desired on the back of the bookmark. For example, a stamped or handwritten greeting, such as "Stamped Especially For You", along with a stamped image that coordinates with the theme of the bookmark.

Stickers can also be used to add color and dimension. When adding stickers — preprinted or made from sticker paper — overlap as desired to add interest.

Finally, the bookmark is assembled and the stamped photo frame sticker with the photo behind it is placed on top of the frame stamped directly onto the cardstock.

Porthole Photo Frame Bookmark

Shown on pages 116 & 118.

- Stamp one porthole frame onto sticker paper and cut out.
- Without re-inking, stamp an identical porthole frame directly onto white cardstock.
- Stamp one anchor with rope onto sticker paper and cut out.
- Place the porthole frame sticker on a cutting mat. Carefully cut out the inside of the porthole frame as shown with a sharp craft knife. This opening in the frame dictates the position of the color-copied photo to be placed behind it.
- Crop the photo to fit the opening in the frame and adhere it in place on the back of the sticker.
- Draw wiggly and dotted lines to create the contour of the shape of the bookmark as shown with blue pigment markers.
- Stamp large "dots" to match the contour of the shape of the bookmark as shown with the eraser-end of a new pencil.
- Place the anchor sticker at the bottom of the bookmark as shown, then place the porthole frame sticker on the front of the bookmark on top of the frame stamped directly onto the cardstock.
- Cut the bookmark out around the contour lines, cutting around the porthole frame.
- Because the bookmark will be used repeatedly, it needs to be laminated and trimmed. This will allow the surface of the bookmark to be wiped clean when necessary.

▲ Porthole Photo Frame Bookmark

▲ Heart Photo Frame Bookmark

Heart Photo Frame Bookmark

Shown on pages 116 & 118.

- Stamp one ribbon heart frame onto sticker paper and cut out.
- Without re-inking, stamp an identical ribbon heart frame directly onto white cardstock.
- Place the ribbon heart frame sticker on a cutting mat. Carefully cut out the inside of the ribbon heart frame as shown with a sharp craft knife. This opening in the frame dictates the position of the color-copied photo to be placed behind it.
- Crop the photo to fit the opening in the frame and adhere it in place on the back of the sticker.
- Draw wiggly lines with curlicues at the ends on the bookmark with colored pigment markers.
- Stamp small colorful hearts on the bookmark as shown.
- Place the ribbon heart frame sticker on the front of the bookmark on top of the frame stamped directly onto the cardstock.
- Cut the bookmark out in any shape as desired, cutting around the ribbon heart frame.
- Because the bookmark will be used repeatedly, it needs to be laminated and trimmed. This will allow the surface of the bookmark to be wiped clean when necessary.

Birthday Cake Photo Frame Bookmark

Shown on pages 116 & 120.

- Stamp one birthday cake frame onto sticker paper and cut out.
- Without re-inking, stamp an identical birthday cake frame directly onto white cardstock.
- Place the birthday cake frame sticker on a cutting mat. Carefully cut out the inside of the birthday cake frame as shown with a sharp craft knife. This opening in the frame dictates the position of the color-copied photo to be placed behind it.
- Crop the photo to fit the opening in the frame and adhere it in place on the back of the sticker. In this instance, the photo was cropped so part of "Mickey Mouse" comes out and over the upper and right sides of the birthday cake frame.
- Draw wiggly lines with curlicues at the ends on the bookmark with colored pigment markers.
- Draw small colorful confetti on the bookmark as shown.
- Place the birthday cake frame sticker on the front of the bookmark on top of the frame stamped directly onto the cardstock.
- Cut the bookmark out in any shape as desired, cutting around the birthday cake frame.

- Because the bookmark will be used repeatedly, it needs to be laminated and trimmed. This will allow the surface of the bookmark to be wiped clean when necessary.

Bow Photo Frame Bookmark

Shown on pages 116 & 120.

- Stamp one bow frame onto sticker paper and cut out.
- Without re-inking, stamp an identical bow frame directly onto white cardstock.
- Place the bow frame sticker on a cutting mat. Carefully cut out the inside of the bow frame as shown with a sharp craft knife. This opening in the frame dictates the position of the color-copied photo to be placed behind it.
- Crop the photo to fit the opening in the frame and adhere it in place on the back of the sticker.
- Draw wiggly lines to create the contour of the shape of the bookmark as shown with pink pigment markers.
- Stamp "Just for You!" on the bookmark as shown.
- Place the bow frame sticker on the front of the bookmark on top of the frame stamped directly onto the cardstock.
- Cut the bookmark out in any shape as desired, cutting around the bow frame.
- Because the bookmark will be used repeatedly, it needs to be laminated and trimmed. This will allow the surface of the bookmark to be wiped clean when necessary.

▲ Bow Photo Frame Bookmark

▲ Birthday Cake Photo Frame Bookmark

Tent
Photo Frame
Bookmark

Shown at right and
on page 116.

- Stamp one tent frame onto
  sticker paper and cut out.

- Without re-inking, stamp
  an identical tent frame directly onto white cardstock.

- Place the tent frame sticker
  on a cutting mat. Carefully
  cut out the inside of the
  tent frame as shown with
  a sharp craft knife. This
  opening in the frame dictates the position of the
  color-copied photo to be
  placed behind it.

- Crop the photo to fit the
  opening in the frame and
  adhere it in place on the
  back of the sticker. In this
  instance, a second photo
  was cropped and added
  to come out of the front of
  the tent frame.

- Draw dashed lines to
  match the contour of the
  shape of the bookmark as
  shown with a brown pig-
  ment marker.

- Stamp grass at the bottom
  of the bookmark as shown.

- Stamp one sitting frog and
  one leaping frog onto sticker paper, cut out, and adhere to the bookmark as
  shown.

- Draw dotted lines behind
  the leaping frog with an
  extrafine-tip brown pigment
  marker to create the illusion
  of movement.

- Place the tent frame sticker
  on the front of the book-

▲ Tent Photo Frame Bookmark

mark on top of the frame
stamped directly onto the
cardstock.

- Cut the bookmark out in
  any shape as desired,
  cutting around the tent
  frame.

- Because the bookmark will
  be used repeatedly, it needs
  to be laminated and trimmed.
  This will allow the surface of
  the bookmark to be wiped
  clean when necessary.

Pencil Cup, Name Tags, Bookmarks, Book Cover, and Candy Bags

PENCIL CUPS
Shown on page 122.

Plastic containers can be purchased in many sizes, but the one shown, used as a pencil cup, measures 2¾" square x 4" high.

To begin, choose a container that will best serve your needs.

Once the container has been chosen, special stamping inks may be needed to insure the stamped images will adhere to the surface of the container. In addition, special ink solvents may be needed for cleaning up mistakes, smears, and general cleanup of rubber stamps.

These special stamping inks generally dry quickly, but make certain to be extremely careful not to smear the ink as you continue stamping.

Make certain to clean each rubber stamp with the appropriate ink solvent after the use of each color.

Simple images can be stamped directly onto the pencil cup. If desired, images can be stamped onto sticker paper, cut out, and adhered to the pencil cup.

Heart Pencil Cup
Shown on page 122.

- Squeeze a small puddle of each color of stamping ink formulated to be used on plastic onto a disposable palette. If desired, ink colors can be mixed at this time.

- Apply the stamping ink onto the rubber stamp with a wedge sponge. Use a different wedge sponge for each color.

- If necessary, lightly blot off excess stamping ink onto a paper towel.

- Practice a few times before actually beginning to stamp on the pencil cup because the rubber stamp may move on the slick surface.

- Stamp hearts directly onto the plastic pencil cup as shown. Be careful not to smear the stamping ink as you continue stamping.

- Immediately cleanup all rubber stamps with the special ink solvent while the stamping ink dries.

NAME TAGS
Shown on page 122.

These name tags can be made in any size, but the one shown measures 4½" wide x 2½" high and are used horizontally. They have been made from sticker paper because it makes the name tag self-adhesive.

To begin, the size of the name tag must be determined. Once the sticker paper has been cut, any background can be applied over the sticker paper as desired.

To begin, a single-lined, or more decorative, border can be drawn on the name tag with colored pigment markers.

Each name tag is personalized with colored pigment markers.

Then, additional detailing can be stamped directly onto the sticker paper name tag or stamped onto sticker paper, cut out, and adhered to the name tag.

When several name tags are desired, it is easiest to work in an assembly-line fashion.

Sunflower Name Tag
Shown on page 122.

- Cut the sticker paper to the size desired for the name tags. One piece of sticker paper is needed for each name tag.

- Draw one wide, wiggly line with an orange pigment marker. Draw another line, just inside the wide line, with a yellow pigment marker.

- Personalize each name tag with a brown pigment calligraphy marker.

- Stamp one sunflower onto sticker paper, cut out, and adhere to the sticker paper name tag as shown.

BOOKMARKS

Shown at right and
on page 122.

These bookmarks can be made in any size and shape. They have been made from cardstock because it can withstand the weight of the stamped embellishments.

To begin, the size and shape of the bookmark must be determined.

Then, additional detailing on the front can be stamped or drawn directly onto the cardstock or stamped onto sticker paper, cut out, and adhered to the cardstock. For this application, embossing is not recommended.

In some instances, detailing may be desired on the back of the bookmark. For example, a stamped or handwritten greeting, such as "Stamped Especially For You", along with a stamped image that coordinates with the theme of the bookmark.

Stickers can also be used to add color and dimension. When adding stickers — preprinted or made from sticker paper — overlap as desired to add interest.

Finally, a hole is punched in the top of the bookmark and a color-coordinated tassel or ribbon is inserted into the hole and secured in place.

School Teacher's Bookmark

Shown at right and
on page 122.

- Draw one wide, wiggly line with a red pigment marker. Draw a thin, dotted line, just inside the wide line, with a blue pigment marker.

- Stamp three apples and one pencil onto sticker paper and cut out.

- Place the apple stickers on the bookmark as shown, then place the pencil sticker.

- Cut the bookmark out in any shape and size as desired.

- Punch a hole in the top of the bookmark and insert a color-coordinated tassel or ribbon into the hole. Secure the tassel or ribbon in place.

- Because the bookmark will be used repeatedly, it needs to be laminated and trimmed. This will allow the surface of the bookmark to be wiped clean when necessary. Laminate the bookmark before the tassel or ribbon is added.

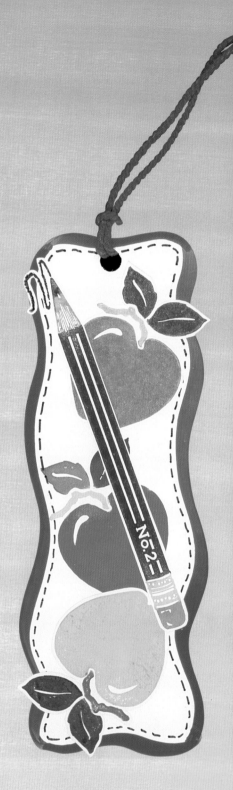

BOOK COVERS

Shown on page 122.

Books in any size can be covered, but the one shown measures 5½" wide x 9" high. The book cover has been made from coated (glossy) paper because it is durable and gives a nice finished look.

To begin, cut a piece of white coated paper that is at least four inches wider and six inches longer than the book (opened with the cover and spine flat).

Once the paper has been cut, any back-ground can be applied over the paper as desired.

Then, additional detailing can be stamped or embossed directly onto the cover or stamped or embossed onto sticker paper, cut out, and adhered to the cover.

Stickers can also be used to add color and dimension. When adding stickers — preprinted or made from sticker paper — overlap as desired to add interest.

With the stamped side of the book cover down, the long sides of the paper are folded in to ⅛" wider than the book. Next, one end is folded in and the front cover of the book inserted into the flap. The paper is pulled around the book, over the spine, and the other end is folded around the back cover of the book. The book is removed to secure the four ends of the folded flaps with an appropriate adhesive. The book is inserted into the book cover and additional stamped embellishments are adhered in place.

School Teacher's Book Cover

Shown on page 122.

- Cut white coated paper to fit appropriately around the book to be covered.

- Stamp "dots" onto the back-ground with the eraser-end of a new pencil.
- Stamp seven apples, two pencils, and one rope frame onto sticker paper and cut out.
- With the stamped side of the book cover down, fold in the long sides of the paper to ⅛" more than the height of the book. Center the open book on the paper. Fold in one end and insert the front cover of the book into the flap. Pull the paper around the book, over the spine, and fold the other end around the back cover of the book. Remove the book and, using the Book Cover Diagram below, secure the four edges of the folded flaps with an appropriate adhesive. Insert the book into the book cover.
- Place the apple and rope frame stickers as shown, then place the pencil stickers.
- Stamp the words "Fifth Grade Room 2" inside the rope frame.

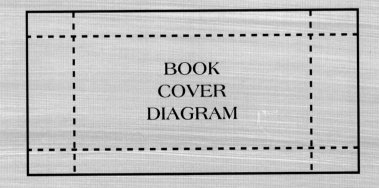

BOOK COVER DIAGRAM

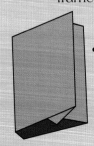

CANDY BAGS
Shown on page 122.

These bags can be made in any size, but the ones shown were made from 3½"-wide cellophane bags with cardstock toppers measuring 3½" wide x 5" high for a folded topper size of 3½" wide x 2½" high.

To begin, the size of the bags must be determined. Once the cardstock for the topper has been cut, any background can be applied over the cardstock.

The cardstock is scored in half width-wise to allow the cardstock to be neatly folded.

Then, additional detailing can be stamped directly onto the cardstock or stamped onto sticker paper, cut out, and adhered to the cardstock.

Words, greetings, or names can be stamped or handwritten on the front of the toppers with colored pigment markers as desired.

Next, fill a 3½"-wide cellophane bag with desired contents and fold the top over to close. The cellophane bag is placed in between the cardstock topper and is stapled to the back of the topper only. The front of the topper is adhered in place with an appropriate adhesive.

When several candy bags are desired, it is easiest to work in an assembly-line fashion.

Jelly Bean Candy Bag
Shown on page 122.

- Cut white coated cardstock 3½" wide x 5" high for a folded topper size of 3½" wide x 2½" high.
- Stamp jelly beans directly onto the background.
- Stamp additional jelly beans onto sticker paper, cut out, and adhere to the cardstock, overlapping as shown.
- Score the cardstock in half width-wise to allow the cardstock to be neatly folded.
- Fill a 3½"-wide cellophane bag with jelly beans and fold the top over to close.
- Place the cellophane bag in between the cardstock topper and staple it to the back of the topper only. Adhere the front of the topper in place with an appropriate adhesive.

Red-Hot Candy Bag
Shown on page 122.

- Cut white coated cardstock 3½" wide x 5" high for a folded topper size of 3½" wide x 2½" high.
- Stamp conversation hearts directly onto the background.
- Stamp additional conversation hearts onto sticker paper, cut out, and adhere to the cardstock, overlapping as shown.
- Score the cardstock in half width-wise to allow the cardstock to be neatly folded.
- Fill a 3½"-wide cellophane bag with red-hots and fold the top over to close.
- Place the cellophane bag in between the cardstock topper and staple it to the back of the topper only. Adhere the front of the topper in place with an appropriate adhesive.

Metric Conversion Chart

INCHES TO MILLIMETRES AND CENTIMETRES

MM-Millimetres   CM-Centimetres

INCHES	MM	CM	INCHES	CM	INCHES	CM
1/8	3	0.9	9	22.9	30	76.2
1/4	6	0.6	10	25.4	31	78.7
3/8	10	1.0	11	27.9	32	81.3
1/2	13	1.3	12	30.5	33	83.8
5/8	16	1.6	13	33.0	34	86.4
3/4	19	1.9	14	35.6	35	88.9
7/8	22	2.2	15	38.1	36	91.4
1	25	2.5	16	40.6	37	94.0
1 1/4	32	3.2	17	43.2	38	96.5
1 1/2	38	3.8	18	45.7	39	99.1
1 3/4	44	4.4	19	48.3	40	101.6
2	51	5.1	20	50.8	41	104.1
2 1/2	64	6.4	21	53.3	42	106.7
3	76	7.6	22	55.9	43	109.2
3 1/2	89	8.9	23	58.4	44	111.8
4	102	10.2	24	61.0	45	114.3
4 1/2	114	11.4	25	63.5	46	116.8
5	127	12.7	26	66.0	47	119.4
6	152	15.2	27	68.6	48	121.9
7	178	17.8	28	71.1	49	124.5
8	203	20.3	29	73.7	50	127.0

YARDS TO METRES

YARDS	METRES	YARDS	METRES	YARDS	METRES	YARDS	METRES	YARDS	METRES
1/8	0.11	2 1/8	1.94	4 1/8	3.77	6 1/8	5.60	8 1/8	7.43
1/4	0.23	2 1/4	2.06	4 1/4	3.89	6 1/4	5.72	8 1/4	7.54
3/8	0.34	2 3/8	2.17	4 3/8	4.00	6 3/8	5.83	8 3/8	7.66
1/2	0.46	2 1/2	2.29	4 1/2	4.11	6 1/2	5.94	8 1/2	7.77
5/8	0.57	2 5/8	2.40	4 5/8	4.23	6 5/8	6.06	8 5/8	7.89
3/4	0.69	2 3/4	2.51	4 3/4	4.34	6 3/4	6.17	8 3/4	8.00
7/8	0.80	2 7/8	2.63	4 7/8	4.46	6 7/8	6.29	8 7/8	8.12
1	0.91	3	2.74	5	4.57	7	6.40	9	8.23
1 1/8	1.03	3 1/8	2.86	5 1/8	4.69	7 1/8	6.52	9 1/8	8.34
1 1/4	1.14	3 1/4	2.97	5 1/4	4.80	7 1/4	6.63	9 1/4	8.46
1 3/8	1.26	3 3/8	3.09	5 3/8	4.91	7 3/8	6.74	9 3/8	8.57
1 1/2	1.37	3 1/2	3.20	5 1/2	5.03	7 1/2	6.86	9 1/2	8.69
1 5/8	1.49	3 5/8	3.31	5 5/8	5.14	7 5/8	6.97	9 5/8	8.80
1 3/4	1.60	3 3/4	3.43	5 3/4	5.26	7 3/4	7.09	9 3/4	8.92
1 7/8	1.71	3 7/8	3.54	5 7/8	5.37	7 7/8	7.20	9 7/8	9.03
2	1.83	4	3.66	6	5.49	8	7.32	10	9.14

Index